MONTGOMERY ROAD

Montgomery Road, Sheffield

Kenwood Lodge

HHC No.12.

Published by Nether Edge Neighbourhood Group

Design and layout by Peter Machan

Printed by A&R Tradeprint

515 Abbeydale Road

0114 258 3434

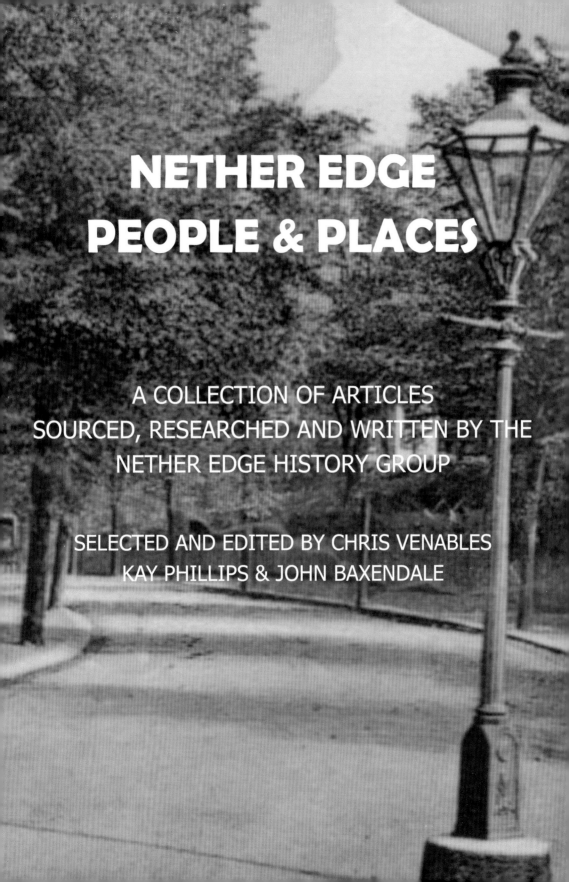

# NETHER EDGE PEOPLE & PLACES

A COLLECTION OF ARTICLES
SOURCED, RESEARCHED AND WRITTEN BY THE
NETHER EDGE HISTORY GROUP

SELECTED AND EDITED BY CHRIS VENABLES
KAY PHILLIPS & JOHN BAXENDALE

# CONTENTS

**Part 1   The Artistic Community**

**Part 2    In Business**

**Part 3  Education**

**Part 4  Wartime**

# INTRODUCTION
## by John Baxendale, Kay Phillips
## & Chris Venables

Like the highly successful *Aspects of Nether Edge* (2017), this book has been produced by members of the Nether Edge History Group, with the support of the Nether Edge Neighbourhood Group. It is also a successor to *They Lived in Sharrow and Nether Edge* (1988). Now thirty years old, this was the work of an earlier History Group; one of whose leading members was Joan Flett, who features in an article in this new book. Where *Aspects* had twelve substantial chapters, *People and Places* consists of articles, of varying length and covering a wide range of subjects - but all are about the people of Nether Edge, the places they lived in and the things they did in their work and leisure time. Underlying all this, we hope, is a sense of how this Victorian suburb made and remade itself as a community from its inception in the 1850s to the present day. The authors too are all local residents with a commitment to that community and an interest in understanding the changes it has gone through.

In its early years, Nether Edge, including some bits then described as Sharrow, was home to some of Sheffield's best known and most influential business families, a species which, with the decline of the family firm, is nearly extinct today. There are plenty of illuminating articles here about those families and the houses they built. But Nether Edge's middle class image has long been tempered by a creative, almost bohemian, reputation, as home to an Art College and to many artists and writers. They have an important place in the book, alongside education, which has always been a concern of Nether Edgers. A number of pieces deal with the impact of historical events on local residents, including the two World Wars, as well as the various campaigning issues, from women's suffrage to the welfare of refugees, in which Nether Edgers habitually become involved.

Community is not only built by campaigns and organisations but also by the ways in which people enjoy themselves together, so we also probe into Nether Edge leisure, from playing snooker to eating out to going to the theatre. Finally, despite the respectable face it could show the world, Victorian Nether Edge was no stranger to scandal and sensation, and we conclude with three examples. But of course we know you will want to read the serious pieces first...

This is, we think, a great dipping-in book, as well as one to get your teeth into. There are short vignettes about people and places here, as well as engaging pieces of close historical research. There are things to learn and things to enjoy – and we hope that here and there you will find the *'well I never knew that'* factor which is one of the attractions of local history. If this book gives you the appetite for more, and the urge to write your own history, look up our Facebook page and come along to our next meeting. You'll be very welcome.

# Part 1
# The Artistic Community

*Nether Edge Postcard, 1908*

# THE SCHOOL OF ART & THE BLUECOAT BUILDING

## Sally Rogers

*View of Sheffield and Brincliffe Quarry by JW McIntyre*

People walking over the brow of Psalter Lane around 1909 might have looked at the building site in the old quarry which had ceased being worked during the last years of the 19th century and wondered what was to be built. The quarry had been owned by the Bluecoat charity and the Salt Box cottages and those on Brincliffe Hill had housed the quarry workers. The new building was intended to accommodate the Bluecoat boys school which was being moved from their building on East Parade behind the Cathedral, a crowded and insanitary central situation, to the new, handsome building in the fresh air of Brincliffe above the city's pollution and smoke. The Bluecoat charity was a 16th century institution which not only educated poor boys in many locations throughout the UK but also provided almshouses for the impoverished elderly. All these charity recipients, including the elderly, wore the distinctive blue clothes, the cloth of which was dyed with the cheap,

*Old Bluecoat School, East Parade.*

woad derived colour.

*Bluecoat School at Psalter Lane*

Despite the healthier situation the Bluecoat regime continued to be harsh and militaristic until 1939 when the army requisitioned the building on Psalter Lane and the boys were distributed to other Sheffield schools and more enlightened educational methods, newly recruited soldiers occupied the premises. In 1945 the building was repurposed as a teacher training college for demobbed soldiers to meet the needs of the post- war baby boom and remained so until 1951.

The Sheffield School of Design was founded in 1843 along with around 200 such schools throughout the UK, following the 1836 Government Select Committee on Art and Manufactures which was convened to support the new industrial growth and see off foreign

*Art School Arundel Street*

competition. Most of these art schools, which even quite small towns such as Chesterfield had, taught the basics of design and a grounding in the local crafts. In 1857 Sheffield School of Art moved to the purpose built premises on Arundel Street in the centre of town from its original home on Glossop Road.   From 1902 to 1925 the Head of the School was Albert Jahn, a metalworker and jeweller, who lived on Meadowbank Avenue and later at Sharrow Mount on Psalter Lane.

In common with these other art schools, Sheffield supplied its local industry with the designers of the florid silverware and its extravagant engraving as well as the memorial (sovereigns, military, poets etc) and the funerary statuary favoured by the Victorians and Edwardians. By the time of the Great Exhibition of 1851, Sheffield was able to make a good showing with such museum favourites as the huge and elaborate, multi-bladed penknife.

*Art School sculpture class 1909*

As well as supporting   local crafts and industries, these art schools, Sheffield included, participated in an older tradition of fine art education, based on Sir Joshua Reynold's dictum when he stressed "the importance of copying   the old masters, and of drawing from the casts after the antique and from the life model"  from his time as one of the founders and first President of the Royal Academy in 1768, our first formal art school. In fact Lorenzo di Medici had encouraged the young artists such as Botticelli and Michelangelo, who were part of his patronage to study his large collection of antique sculpture, and the idea that such study was fundamental in the training of artists was not abandoned until after World War II.

These two strands of creativity were to sit uneasily with one another for at least another century before they were combined by adventurous artists such as Peter Blake and Richard Hamilton to dynamic effect. After the School of Arts and Crafts was bombed in 1940 the classes were held for some years in whatever spaces could be found in and around Arundel and Norfolk Streets before the college was reopened at the Bluecoat School site on Psalter Lane in 1951.

*Derek and Dorothy Sellars*

Derek Sellars and Dorothy Haworth were students in the first year of the relocated art school at Psalter Lane in 1951. They remember that it was the "cleaner" subjects  such as drawing, painting and printmaking that moved and messy stone carving , clay work etc  continued in and around the central sites in makeshift accommodation.

Both Derek and Dorothy completed the 4 years undergraduate courses and Dorothy pursued further study at the prestigious Slade School of Art whilst Derek was accepted onto the post graduate course at the internationally renowned Royal College of Art. However, the Royal College was reluctant to defer Derek's National Service and so in 1956 he did his 2 years in the RAF near Liverpool. *"I managed to get the RAF to let me have one day a week in the Sculpture Department of Liverpool College of Art and free support from the head of sculpture and I was astonished by their massive number of "classical" plastercasts which students spent a lot of time copying, like all of Britain's Art Schools – except Sheffield where only one piece was left after the bombing. I have a somewhat romantic  theory that our college became leadingly inventive because we were spared a gang of plastercasts...."*

The newly established Art College at Psalter Lane continued with a modern and  forward looking agenda, awarding students the 2 year Intermediate qualification  followed  by  the  National  Diploma  in  Design  (NDD), Silversmithing  being still an important course as before, alongside drawing, painting and sculpture.

Growing up in the area I was fascinated by the beatnik looking students, the girls with their straight, Juliet Greco hair, stripy jumpers and black stockings, very different from the perms and twinsets of the time. Other children I knew weren't allowed anywhere near  them but my ambition was to be one of them when I grew up. It was during this time around 1957, I think, that the new, one storey block was built at right angles to the old building, to house sculpture, ceramics and industrial design. Then, to complete a square, another low rise building appeared opposite the main frontage of the old building, and this was for an expanded and modern printmaking dept.

When I joined as a pre Dip student in 1964 (the 1 or 2 year pre- diploma course was later superseded by Art Foundation, a diagnostic and taster course for school leavers) it was a small, cosy set up utilising some decrepit buildings behind the main

*Dorothy Sellars 'The Show'*

college, left over from Bluecoat and army days as well as some rooms down the road in the long, stone building next to the bus stop belonging to Nether Edge Hospital and across the road in a coach house belonging to Nether Edge Grammar School (junior art school). By this time the student style was hippie and they met with the same disdain as the beatniks had in the fifties. A notice on the door of the Union pub banned entry to long-haired (men) and scruffy dressers.

George Melly captured the atmosphere of art schools and art students at the time: "the refuge of the bright but unacademic, the talented, the non-

conformist, the lazy, the inventive and the indecisive". The college was relaxed with plenty of individual attention from the staff who were practising artists and craftspeople as well as lecturers.

Derek and Dorothy Sellars had completed their studies, married and joined the staff as lecturers in sculpture and in their well equipped studio at home they produced their artwork which was regularly exhibited nationally. They raised a family and are long time residents of Nether Edge and in 2018 they will have been married for 58 years.

*Derek Sellars 'Signpost to Spidean Mialach'*

To me, a one time student of Derek and Dorothy, the tone from that relaxed time is invoked by the arrival of the grey education committee school meals van which used to call daily with its delivery to the small canteen, as it did its rounds of the Sheffield schools. The many small Art Schools were still run by the local education authorities.

Following the recommendations of the Coldstream Report of 1960 into the state of art education in the UK, some colleges in major centres were able to expand including Sheffield College of Art. It now entered a dynamic phase and the Diploma in Art and Design, (Dip AD), replaced the NDD. Amongst the report's recommendations was more emphasis on the history of art and the introduction of liberal studies in order to encourage a broader cultural awareness. This had the happy effect of expanding students' education beyond the practical acquisition of skills. We were encouraged to read, visit galleries and other places of interest, listen to a range of music and there was valuable exchange between the lecturers and students. At 17 I was fascinated by Derek and Dorothy's detailed account of their bus journey from Athens to Delphi. Cheaper air and train travel allowed more students the novelty of backpacking around Europe to see first hand art works which their rich young 18th predecessors had seen on their Grand Tours.

The Robbins Report of 1963 on the future of Higher Education ushered in the reorganisation of technical, teacher training and art colleges and in 1969 Sheffield College of Art merged with these colleges to form Sheffield Polytechnic. The school of art expanded to become one of the largest and most influential in the UK. At this time the new tall block was built and more specialist courses were added to the Sheffield Dip AD list, now about to change to a BA as the Polytechnic became Sheffield Hallam University. The College of Art had already become a prime player in the sixties by allowing space, through a flexible examining regime, for interdisciplinary activities to include music, performance, film and photography, as well as teaching the traditional skills. This creative dynamic, shared with the other major art institutions, was largely instrumental in shaping the aesthetics of the 'swinging sixties' and helped the UK to be pre-eminent in the world of design and culture at that time.

Students were mostly resident in and around Nether Edge, being of that first post war cohort to leave their home to take up appropriate places at university or college in another town, aided by a small but liveable maintenance grant. Art students had come from their small local art school where they'd completed their Pre- Dip or Foundation courses to join the expanded colleges where they could specialise in their chosen area; Sheffield now attracted students interested in silversmithing from all over the country. The largely positive social upheaval caused by so many of the baby boom generation leaving home for the first time was especially exhilarating in art schools. Committed young men who had struggled against family

*New buildings at the Art College*

expectations to take up a 'manly' occupation were likely to rub shoulders with young women whose old fashioned parents reckoned a bit of water colour painting was just the thing before marriage. By 1968 the college was, in keeping with the time, alive with political activism especially feminism.

Then as now, there were many large but difficult to maintain and heat Victorian and Edwardian houses, some neglected and in poor condition. Sub-divided into flats and bedsits often by unscrupulous landlords, they were conveniently scattered around Nether Edge; almost the whole of Sheldon Rd and Machon Bank, the Kenwood area as well as the steep roads from the college down to Hunters Bar.

Flats and bedsits were furnished and decorated from the house clearance businesses that sprung up in the slum demolition areas of Sharrow and London Rd. Saturdays were spent picking up chenille curtains, marble topped washstands, religious and sentimental genre paintings and photographs, plaster statuettes of pastoral figures amongst other Victorian paraphernalia, for a few shillings. Clothes too, feather boas and fox furs, 1930s dresses, long 1920s scarves, interesting hats, picked up cheaply and worn eccentrically. Bits of pre WW1 military uniforms seemed to turn up too, presumably from volunteer armies such as the Boer War, and disappeared into attics. The army surplus stores were also popular hunting grounds for cheap greatcoats, desert boots and khaki kit bags for our arty equipment.

At the graduation show held at the Psalter Lane site in 1967 the table from which the diplomas were handed out was covered in a large Union Jack and the trendier boys wore the Sergeant Pepper inspired red military jackets with jeans, long scarves and hair and droopy moustaches.

*Sally Rogers making hats*

The Union Hotel may not have been welcoming but the Banner Cross Hotel and Stag benefitted from staff and student custom. A nip over the wall at the corner of Psalter Lane and Brincliffe Hill and down the opposite gennel to Ecclesall Rd meant spending a good part of the lunch hour at the Banner Cross pub. Wednesday evenings were spent at the Polish Club, Ecclesall Rd where we danced to R&B, Motown and Soul music. Later on this evening moved to Shades, a club in the basement of the Greystones cinema. Turnups on Nether Edge Rd was also a popular dance venue until the local residents finally got fed up and it closed in the early 80s. The Raven on Fitzwilliam St, a bit off the usual Nether Edge stamping ground was always packed out with art and university students in its large, club style room with a stage at one end where college bands were welcome to play. It also attracted students with the traditional Thursday night hand out of black pudding and sandwiches, a Sheffield custom from the days when Little Mesters paid out the wages from the safe of the local pub, and the landlord, keen to keep the workers drinking and spending extended their hospitality with these titbits. Food and clothes weren't as cheap and available then so students were glad of the second hand clothes options and places like steel workers' early morning cafes where they could get a slice of bread and dripping, a pint mug of tea and five Park Drive cigarettes for a shilling or so when they came off the night shift. Some of the male students augmented their grants by joining the night workers in steel works or bakeries before a day at college; sometimes helping to support family back home.

This creative stew of UK art schools (the 200 created across the country in the 19th century was the highest density per population in Europe if not the world) famously produced some internationally regarded artists and designers....and musicians. Psalter Lane's alumni include Annie Bindon-Carter who started Painted Fabrics in 1923; the abstract expressionist painter John Hoyland, who joined the cohort of northern actors, writers, and musicians whose accents were a novelty in the fashionable world of 1950s London, but de rigueur in the 1960s; David Mellor whose cutlery and silverware as well as industrial design is well known everywhere, and Nick Park of Wallace and Grommit fame. There are many practising artists and craftspeople and art teachers/instructors educated at Psalter Lane now working in and around Sheffield.

I graduated in 1969 and entered the post-graduate Art Teachers Certificate course at the Institute of Education, London University before returning to Sheffield and starting a career backstage at the newly opened Crucible Theatre alongside some fellow graduates. Later I was able to combine free-lance theatrical millinery with teaching and recently retired from the University of Leeds where I was employed in the Dept of Performance as demonstrator/technician in costume. Inevitably I encountered other Psalter Lane  graduates on the staff there.

The Psalter Lane site had become outdated and too expensive to maintain. The site was sold to developers and Sheffield Institute of Art, as it became known, moved in 2008 to newly built premises at the main Pond St site, and in 2016 into the old post office building in Fitzalan Square, where it has found a congenial, spacious and independent home. The area where we used to queue at the counters for stamps has been converted to an airy and elegant exhibition area with a café; a proper 19th century Art school! The Psalter Lane site has been fully developed with houses, the newer art blocks demolished and the old Bluecoat/Art School building, surprisingly not listed, converted to luxury apartments, stands on Bluecoat Rise.

*Psalter Lane closure*

15

# JOYCE HIMSWORTH, SILVERSMITH
## Sarah Matthews and Kay Phillips

Joyce Himsworth built her reputation as a fine craftswoman in the early and mid-twentieth century. Born at Machon Bank on 19th August 1905, Joyce was welcomed into the world by her father Joseph Beeston Himsworth, craftsman and artist, and Dora Himsworth, a schoolteacher. For the purpose of this article, her story begins in 1908, when her father and brother bought land on Chelsea Road and started work on the building of two adjacent houses, numbers 29 and 31. The Himsworths were keen to leave their personal mark on the properties, and at the age of just four or five, Joyce laid a foundation stone at number 31 bearing her initials, a touch that can still be seen near the front door of the home. Perhaps it was the feeling that the family's residence at the property would be long-lasting that prompted Joyce's father to include a handmade stained glass window for the front door, decorated with a flattering line painting of his young daughter in profile, signed and dated 1910. In later years, the extension built on the side of the property meant that Joyce was never too far from her father as she lived in the main house, connected to Joseph in the adjoining building by a shared door.

It is not surprising that Joyce became immersed in the world of manufacturing from an early age. The Himsworths had links to the Stokes family, owners of one of the country's most established paint manufacturing businesses, through the marriage of Joyce's aunt Sabrina Himsworth to Robert Stokes in the late 1800s. More directly, the creative influence of her father, a fellow craftsperson, is likely to have encouraged her to discover her skill. She was said to have been taught by her father from an early age and made her first spoon aged five. This early exposure set her on a path of pursuing her own line of work, eventually making a name for herself as a maker and designer. Her close relationship with her father and their shared passion for their work was what brought them together in a professional capacity.

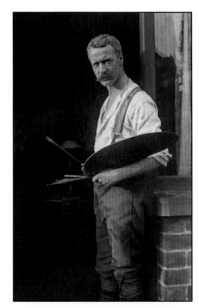

*Joseph Beeston Himsworth (c 1910-20)*

Growing up, Joyce had been taught how to make all sorts of pieces by her father, from spoons to jewellery. In 1925, they took the step of registering a joint mark at the Sheffield Assay Office, a mark that Joyce would continue to use on the work she produced as an independent designer and silversmith.

In the early years of her career, Joyce studied at Sheffield School of Art, now the Sheffield Institute of Arts at Sheffield Hallam University. She progressed

*Joyce Himsworth (right) 1940s*

to the Central School of Arts and Crafts in London before returning to Sheffield to work. 1925 seems to have been a significant year, as she also became a member of the Sheffield Artcrafts Guild. As a Guild member she became involved with the education of the budding craftspeople of Sheffield, spending time as a lecturer at Sheffield Trades Technical Society, Rotherham School of Art and the Chesterfield School of Art.

Alongside these teaching commitments, she continued to progress in her own career, gaining a City and Guilds of London 1st Class Technological Certificate and first place in the country in enamelling. Further achievements included first prize in national competitions at the Worshipful Company of Goldsmiths in 1937 and 1938, another prize in a competition run by the Worshipful Company of Armorers and Braziers, and a range of recognitions for her design and workmanship from the Sheffield Silver Trades.

Joyce Himsworth's areas of expertise were self-confessed at the top of her letterhead, where she listed 'church and domestic silverware, presidential badges, christening gifts and spoons'. Her influences were far reaching and included everything from Egyptian, Celtic and more contemporary Art Deco designs, and pieces ranged from small and intricate jewellery to large functional bowls. It was perhaps this diversity, as well as the affordability and fashionable design of her work, which contributed to her commercial success. The popularity of Joyce's work was reflected in the demand for its display. It was exhibited in various places, including the Red Rose Guild of Craftsmen exhibition at the Whitworth Art Gallery in Manchester, 1951, where she showed over fifteen pieces of her own. She also took part in an exhibition of 'The Work of the Modern Designer-Craftsmen', arranged by the

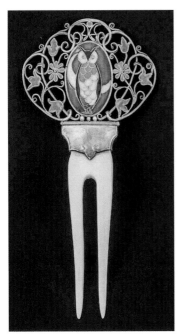

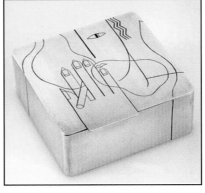

*Examples of Joyce's work*

Crafts Centre of Great Britain for the Arts Council in 1955, putting her at the cutting edge of her craft even in the final years of her active career.

As a craftswoman, Joyce Himsworth was recognised not just within her field, but also by the public at both a local and national level. In 1933, The Sheffield Telegraph dubbed her *'one of our modern masters in the manipulation of gold and silver'.* Goldsmiths' Journal was equally complimentary in 1937, praising her for the ability to combine, *'technical excellence of design with an appreciation of what should appeal'.*

This praise did not prevent Joyce from challenging the Goldsmiths' Company on the matter of recognition for female makers. On the 22nd July 1945 she wrote a letter to the Company making the case for women makers to be given status equal to that of men. She wrote;

*'Dear Mr Hughes,*

*Regarding the problems and the future of goldsmiths and silversmiths I should like to suggest , that in whatever plans are made to assist craftsmen, exactly the same may apply to craftswomen, This may appear to some an unnecessary appeal, and perhaps at the moment, the proportion of women to which it might apply is small,. Nevertheless, the old (and now senseless) idea still persists in some quarters, that a woman, whatever her achievements, should not partake of the full privileges or honours for so* many centuries reserved for, and thus assisting the man, in his business career.

*It seems to me that the present (particularly after the equal compulsion and achievements of women in so many spheres during the last few years) is a time of great opportunity for the Government and such bodies as the Goldsmiths' Company, to give equal opportunity, remuneration and status to apprentices, designers and craft-workers (of whichever sex). This should form a part of all plans decided upon in connection with suggestions already made for training, for a Design Centre, and for an Associate Livery.'*

This was a very radical proposal to an extremely conservative organisation. The last woman to be apprenticed as a jeweller before the 20th century had been Elizabeth Reilly in 1781, and she never took up her 'freedom' on completion of the apprenticeship. No women were admitted to the Goldsmiths' Company after 1845; they could attend balls but were excluded from all Company business. Four decades would pass before Joyce's demands were realised, but at least she lived to see the change. The first woman to gain her freedom by service in more than 200 years was Wendy Cooke in 1983. She had been apprenticed as an engraver to the firm Gerrard.

Joyce exhibited her work in the UK, Europe, America, Canada and Australia, during a long and successful career. One of her most significant commissions was for a pair of lily vases and two chalices for Westminster Cathedral. She retired in the 1960s.

Although Joyce is best known for her design and craft work, her passion was also evident in other areas of her personal life. She was a strict and committed vegetarian and a proud member of the Vegetarian Society. Her tendency to break norms and to live by her own principles can also be seen in her interest in left-wing politics, particularly in Russian Communism. She was a member of the British-Soviet Friendship Society and the British Peace Committee and her political influences were sometimes visible in her work. Quite remarkably, one such occasion when she was able to use her craft to political ends was in response to the German invasion of Russia in 1943. Joyce became part of a group of makers involved in the creation of a stainless steel, enamelled casket containing the signatures of Sheffield women on parchment. It was sent to the women of Stalingrad commending their 'courage and sacrifice in the face of overwhelming odds'.

Joyce had not taken the usual path of marriage and family life and, in the years before she died, she was joined at 31 Chelsea Road by Esther Wood, a lady who had previously been housekeeper and nanny to the Stokes family on Kingfield Road. She also found company in David Sier and his wife Angela, who helped to look after her as she became increasingly frail. Joyce remained at her childhood home in Nether Edge until her death in 1989. A display of her exceptional work can still be found in Sheffield's Millennium Gallery.

**Sources.**

*'The Work and Legacy of the Sheffield Arts & Crafts Guild'*, Silver Studies, 2008, p47-52. Conroy, Rachel.
The Goldsmiths' Review 2016-17, p16-17. *'Women and the Goldsmiths Company',* Sophia Tobin.

---

# ANNIE BINDON CARTER, ARTIST

# Malcolm Leary

Annie Clara Bindon Carter is best remembered as the founder of a Sheffield textile company which became an internationally known fashion house. She was the inspiration behind Painted Fabrics, an initiative that brought great benefit to injured servicemen in the aftermath of the First World War.

Born in 1883 in Nottingham, the young Annie attended the Ladies' Moravian School in Ockbrook, Derby, where the Moravian Church's Protestant values would have been intrinsic to her education. Its strong moral emphasis on service to others may help to explain her later commitment to the Painted Fabrics project.  On leaving school she obtained a scholarship to the Sheffield School of Art where, as a talented student, she won a prize for her mural decorations. Annie also received awards for her silver and textile designs whilst working for several firms in Sheffield and London.

In 1909, at the age of 26, she married freemason Geoffrey Cecil Carter, owner of Carter and Sons, manufacturing chemists in Attercliffe. Annie spent thirty five years of her life in Nether Edge. Her home was 'Kingfield House', which Geoffrey had purchased for his wife and their two daughters in 1933.

It was a large house with grounds occupying the area between St Andrew's Road and the narrow passageway adjacent to number 53 Kingfield Road. Unfortunately Geoffrey died in 1940; he had fought in Mesopotamia during the First World War and was injured in action. He became increasingly incapacitated, to the extent that he

*St Andrew's church with Kingfield House*

was paraplegic in later life. Annie continued to occupy the house until she died in 1968. 'Kingfield House' was demolished in 1968/9 and replaced with a new housing development.

## The Rehabilitation of Men Returning from the War

After the First World War (1914-18) many young soldiers, some severely disabled, returned home without any hope of future employment and with a life of despair and destitution in front of them. Annie Bindon Carter refused to believe that these men were fit for nothing. From the beginning of the War virtually no support had been available in terms of accommodation, facilities, equipment and above all ideas on what to do to help the thousands returning from the Front. Led by Annie, a small group of young, female art students from Sheffield Art College approached Colonel Vincent, head of the Wharncliffe War Hospital at Middlewood, for permission to visit severely maimed soldiers. Annie believed they could speed their rehabilitation if they gave them an interest to relieve their boredom. Phyllis Lawton, who along with Dorothy Carter (Annie's sister), Edith Jagger and a few other friends answered Annie Bindon Carter's call, wrote-

*"It was in 1916 that Annie Carter asked me to her home to discuss, along with other School of Art students, the possibility of forming an Art class at Wharncliffe War Hospital. The idea was just as an occupation for the wounded when they were able to move about. We decided to give it a try. A committee was formed of which I was one and we all agreed to take certain materials of our own to start with and look out some of our stencils and cut some simple designs as a start. We were able to go on three afternoons a week from 2 till 4pm... It was a great success from the start."*

The classes were held in the hospital dining room on long trestle tables and in addition to stencilling, the men did watercolour painting, black and white work, pen painting, basket weaving and bead making.

## Work not Charity

Although the art class project began as a way of filling time for the wounded, Annie soon realised that much more was needed if they were to have any sense of purpose or prospect of future employment. This change apparently resulted from a chance encounter in 1916 with Corporal William Wallwork, an ex-serviceman from Bolton. Before the War he had worked as a butcher but there was no possibility that he could ever return to his old job:

*'He had suffered terribly in the war; he had been burned by liquid fire and both hands had been amputated. One arm was off at the elbow, the other arm finished at the wrist. His face was also burned. He was wandering in the grounds of the hospital in a distraught state, very depressed, with his cuffs stuck in the pockets of his great coat. When she suggested that he might like to join her art class he scoffed at the idea of drawing without hands. His face had a solemn expression and as he pulled his deformed hands from his pocket, his strong words were "What can I do with these!" holding up the bandaged stumps. After a good deal of persuasion, he eventually came to the classes. Mrs Carter was profoundly touched by this incident and immediately set about devising a plan. She began by tying a brush to the stump of one of his arms, then cutting out stencils. She taught him to paint, first on paper and afterwards on cushion covers through the stencils. She knew little about human anatomy but the specially designed tool at least enabled him to do some of the work. 'I was in despair, life did not hold anything worth living for, but this work showed me that there was at least something useful I could do. It gave me hope and courage.'*

(Bolton Journal and Guardian 12th November 1926)

The women artists saw uses for the skills and techniques that they themselves had developed; the challenge was to pass them on to others. At first this seemed impossible because severely disabled servicemen had been accepted largely on an ad hoc basis for treatment at institutions in Sheffield from 1916 onwards. Many, like Corporal Wallwork, were in a desperate situation. Battle weary and struggling with both physical and psychological problems, they were men who had seen too much during the conflict. Some were so badly affected by what were then called 'fits' they had to be treated as best they could by Annie's totally untrained helpers in a darkened room.

Annie and her colleagues managed to develop many devices which helped the men to do the work themselves, of which they were justly proud. They soon began to show ability in the work and in doing things neatly. The first sale of their work was held in the lower Cutlers' Hall in Sheffield; it was opened by the Countess Fitzwilliam and, to everyone's relief, was a great success. At the sale a long strip poster was put across the stall of Sheffield work.

*Men at work painting fabric*

ALL WORK GUARANTEED DONE BY WOUNDED SOLDIERS AT WHARNCLIFFE WAR HOSPITAL

There was also a fine poster done by Charles Sargeant Jagger the famous sculptor; his sister Edith was one of the helpers. The fledgling organisation was initially known as the Soldiers and Sailors Mutual Association (S.A.S.M.A.). It had a formal committee and from the start Annie recognised the need to enlist the support of people with influence; Maud Countess Fitzwilliam and Earl Haig were two generous advocates and benefactors.

## A Moral Necessity

It was at the Sheffield sale that Annie Carter first spoke publicly about the possibility of forming an industry for badly disabled men, declaring that she was willing to dedicate her life to such a project. Her motto was 'Work not Charity', and it was therefore a 'Moral Necessity' that a legitimate private company should be launched. She realised that many of the men would never be robust again and that some light occupations would be all that could ever be expected of them, but they would have some dignity.

Annie's name has rightly become synonymous with the company which she founded, aided by Phyllis, Dorothy and Edith who were responsible for designing the sought-after patterns. Some reflected the style of William Morris and the Arts and Crafts movement but there were other contemporary influences. Years later Edith wrote;

*'From the beginning the style of Painted Fabrics designs was very varied, but the bold and brilliant colour combinations and the fluid use of fabric in their designs for clothing were very much in tune with the period, showing the*

*influence of Fauves painters such as Matisse and Dufy and the excitement of the Oriental, inspired by Diaghilev's Ballets Russes'.*

Oriental curtain designs made by Painted Fabrics were on sale in Manchester at Messrs. Goodall as early as 1918. All of the goods produced were of high quality and Painted Fabrics quickly became an internationally recognised fashion house, supported by nobility and royalty and holding sales and exhibitions in prestigious venues and homes. At all of these the men were the ones proudly displaying and selling the products they had made. By this time (1918) the creative work was being done in newly adapted workshops in the centre of Sheffield.

## The Painted Fabrics Company

A limited company was established in 1923, when land and 'hutments' were leased at a former Women's Auxiliary Army Corps (WAAC) camp at Norton. It was formally opened by Princess Mary in 1925 and Annie Bindon Carter was awarded an M.B.E. in 1926 in recognition of her work. The Company had a formal structure: H.M Queen Elizabeth, the Queen Mother was its Patron along with H.R.H. the Princess Royal. The Company's four Vice-Patrons were all titled. Business leaders, captains of industry and local dignitaries served on the Board of Directors, with Geoffrey Carter as its Honorary Secretary. The Company's Management Committee included The Bishop of Sheffield, Sir Charles Clifford and Sir John Rothenstein; Annie was the Committee's Honorary Secretary. All gave their services for free.

*The Norton Painted Fabrics Community*

Over the next 15 years the company thrived. Some of the hutments were converted into homes for the men and their families, others were turned into workshops. In 1928 ten houses were built as Haig Memorial Homes and a community developed with gardens, allotments, social clubs and events. The block of houses was built in the form of flats, so that the men without legs could occupy the ground floor and those without hands the upper storey. All the men at Painted Fabrics were described as 100% disabled, this meant that they had lost two limbs and had a full pension, so they didn't have to work very long hours. Up to 67 men were employed at one time. Some stayed for a short period: others spent their whole working lives there.

The site became a place where employees' families created their own thriving community. They acted as guides for visitors and it was commented that no Royal event in Sheffield was complete without a visit to Painted Fabrics. As the enterprise expanded so did the range of products, all of which were of very high quality. Goods on sale included handkerchiefs, scarves, shawls, dresses, lingerie, furnishing fabrics, curtains (including theatre curtains) and church fabrics. Prices reflected the high quality of the materials used and prestigious shops like Claridges and Liberty in London stocked the Painted Fabrics range.

During the Second World War (1939-45) the workshops were taken over for making aircraft parts but Painted Fabrics resumed its work in 1950. Unfortunately it was never able to regain the success that it had enjoyed pre-war. The last sale took place at the Cutlers' Hall in 1958 and the business was formally wound up in 1959. Maud Fitzwilliam, of its most loyal patrons and Annie Bindon Carter's friend, wrote:-

*"15th February 1957*

*THE CROFT, MALTON, NORTH YORKSHIRE*

*My very dear friend, dearest Binnie,*

*Bless you and thank you for your lovely letter, all most interesting and I loved hearing about Painted Fabrics. It is sad it has come to an end - but what a truly wonderful work you have completed, and so many lives you have made happy, and who, without you would have been so sad and no interest left, with nothing to do and nothing to look forward to accomplishing and producing something worthwhile. The curtains [made at Painted Fabrics] still hang at Wentworth Castle and here the bedspread to match, which all came from the shop at Chesterfield Street. What happy days were the exhibitions at Wentworth and No 4 Grosvenor Square and then at Claridges to which the Princess Royal drew the King's attention. I do congratulate you from the depths of my heart. Bless you and much love.*

*Maud Fitz, Countess Fitzwilliam."*

**Postscript**

Annie Bindon Carter died in September 1968 at the age of 85. The Painted Fabrics site on Little Norton Lane was redeveloped and new sheltered housing replaced the Haig Memorial Homes. A blue plaque commemorating Painted Fabrics marks the site. In 2016 Weston Park Museum hosted an exhibition celebrating her life and work. Costumes, fabrics and designs from the Painted Fabrics Company were displayed, along with books purchased for Sheffield University Library with a £1000 donation from Annie.

With grateful thanks to Malcolm Leary for providing content for this article. His book, *'Painted with Pride: The Forgotten Story of How One Woman Taught the Broken Men of WW1 to Live Again'* (2016), is available via www.rmcbooks.co.uk.

---

# THE DRABBLE FAMILY, AUTHORS

# Kay Phillips and John Austin

Two of England's most significant female authors, Dame Antonia Byatt and Dame Margaret Drabble, spent their early years living on Meadow Bank Avenue. The two sisters have won numerous awards for literature, having written over forty novels and short story collections and more than a dozen non-fiction books, including biographies, literary essays and editions of The Oxford Companion to English Literature. This overview draws from some of their writings to illustrate both positive and negative aspects of their lives during the period 1936-1954. Sources used include Margaret Drabble's 'The Pattern in the Carpet' and 'The Peppered Moth' and A.S Byatt's 'Ragnarok' and 'Sugar'. Other material has been drawn from published interviews and videos with the two authors. We are also grateful to Margaret Drabble for contributing personal photographs and recollections to the Meadow Bank Avenue History Project.

## The Parents

John Frederick Drabble and Kathleen Marie Bloor, both born in 1907, began living on Meadow Bank Avenue in 1936. Initially the young couple and their first child, Antonia Susan lived at number 38. They left the city in 1939, the year in which Margaret was born, to escape the threat of German bombing. The family evacuated to Pontefract, returning to the Avenue after the War to live at number

36. The pair of houses had been bought with money provided by John's paternal Grandfather. It was quite common for purchasers to buy a pair of semi-detached houses so that income could be generated by renting out one, or even both, of the properties. Built at the beginning of the twentieth century, these were good, solid Victorian villas in a quiet, suburban environment.

John and Marie (she used her middle name rather than Kathleen) had grown up in Conisbrough, where John Drabble's family ran a small sweet-making business. Both had done very well at school. They had attended Mexborough Grammar and then progressed to Cambridge; Marie, a scholarship student, went to Newnham College to read English and John to Downing College to read Law. His father initially failed to see why his son should want to go to Cambridge so John had worked as a travelling salesman in the family business for a while before he took up a place. They were both the first in their families to go to university.

**A.S.Byatt (top) and Margaret Drabble (above)**

The young couple married after university and went on to have four children, three daughters and a son. Antonia Susan (always referred to as Susan in the family) was born in 1936, Margaret in 1939, Helen in 1945 and Richard in 1949. The family would have been quite comfortably off once John was a fully qualified lawyer and he enjoyed success both in his legal career and military service. During the War he served in the RAF and was distinguished as a Squadron Leader. He was away from his family for most of the duration of the war, including a period of service in Italy.

Susan had spent three years with her father before the War. Margaret, born in 1939, didn't really get to know him until he returned from service in 1945. In Ragnarok Susan writes of her 'steady fear' that her father would not return from the war.

*'Instead, one night, after midnight, when the blackout was still over the windows, he did come back, unexpected and unannounced. The child was woken, and there he was, his red-gold hair shining, gold wings on his tunic, his arms out to hold her as she leaped at him'.*

Returning to civilian life, John resumed his legal career. He was also politically active and firmly on the left. In 1945, he stood as Labour candidate in the Conservative Hallam constituency; he won 38.5% of the vote but lost. Undaunted he tried again in the Huddersfield West constituency in 1955 but again had to accept defeat. During this time he was rising through the legal profession, becoming a barrister and QC in the 1950s.

Meanwhile Marie had worked as a teacher in a local school, leaving the profession when she had the first of her children in 1936. This was the norm at that time. During the War women were recruited to fill teaching posts left vacant by men who had signed up for military service and Marie was employed at Mexborough Grammar School. Post-war, she engaged in some writing and tutoring of individual pupils but, as the wife of a professional man and mother of children, was unable to pursue a career of her own outside of the home. She was an aspirational woman and Sheffield was not going to satisfy those aspirations and so, after John became a Circuit Judge, it was Marie who steered the family south to live in Sevenoaks, away from provincial life in the North.

Each of the four Drabble children would go on to achieve academic success at Cambridge and considerable renown in their chosen careers. Susan (A.S.Byatt) and Margaret have made major contributions to English literature; Helen Langdon is a respected, well-published art historian and Richard has followed in his father's profession to become a barrister and highly-regarded QC.

**Positive Childhood Memories**

In an article in the Sunday Times Magazine of 1st October 2006 Margaret described Meadow Bank Avenue as follows;

*John Drabble with Antonia and Helen outside number 36*

'We lived in a semi-detached Edwardian house with a cellar and an attic, in a neighbourhood called Nether Edge, only a couple of miles from the city centre. Nether Edge was indeed an edge: Sheffield is full of edges. Our road was called Meadow Bank Avenue, and even at the age of six I recognised that there was something special about it. Its entrance led through a gate marked Private Road into an oval lime-tree-lined loop with a pseudo village green in the middle. This gate was closed one day in the year to maintain its status. I discovered many years later that what we all knew as 'the green' had been called the 'Pleasure Ground' when the estate was designed in the 1890s; it was supposed to encourage a communal spirit and it did. Bonfire nights were very communal: almost, by the modest standards of the day, orgiastic.*

*I remember sitting on the wall of the green across the road from our house and being allowed to join in the games of older children. I particularly admired the older boy next door, from the other half of our semi: he was a red-haired hero who, like me, had a stammer. My mother coached him for his Cambridge entrance, and in later life he became a distinguished translator of Lacan, Foucault and Sartre, and the author of a startling homoerotic novel. I still find that evolution surprising, though there is no reason why Meadow Bank Avenue should not have fostered such an unusual talent.'*

Both A.S.Byatt and Margaret Drabble have returned to Meadow Bank Avenue and have written and spoken about their childhood experiences of living there. Antonia (known in the family by her middle name Susan), also described the garden at Meadow Bank Avenue in her book, Ragnarok. She pictures a small, thin, asthmatic child gardening with the father, reshaping the garden and building terraces into its steep slope. John Drabble had done exactly that; a photograph on p30, supplied by Margaret Drabble, captures him in the process of terracing the back garden down to the boundary wall on Machon Bank Road.

The following extract from Ragnarok conveys the strong bond between Susan and her father.

She describes his terraces, '*holding in flowerbeds, with lilies, Shirley poppies, rose bushes, lavender, thyme and rosemary. He made a pool from an old stone sink, in which swam tadpoles and a stickleback... It was a pretty garden in its newness, despite the soot in the air. The thin child loved her father, and loved the garden, and wheezed.*'

*Margaret Drabble on the wall of Meadow Bank Avenue (1950s)*

In a 2008 interview with The Guardian newspaper, Margaret Drabble described her father as a handsome man with red hair and freckles, a clear-cut friendly face and slightly abstracted gaze. He was 'an extraordinarily fair-minded, generous-spirited man' in his role as a QC. As a father 'he worked grindingly hard. My parents almost never went out and we were always being told to shut up. Yet he was an affectionate father and....he would unbend and give us his full attention when on holiday.'

In her book, 'The Pattern in the Carpet', Margaret Drabble describes the family home in which she grew up in the 1940s, giving the impression that it was rather dull, with little in the way of decoration or ornaments and few pictures on the walls. It was very quiet (because their father worked on his legal papers in the evenings) and there were few toys but many books. John Drabble did tapestry in the evenings when he wasn't working. A picture emerges of a subdued household in which the children were expected to keep themselves occupied.  Their mother shopped locally in Nether Edge and there are memories of the local butchers with its hanging carcasses, the delights of the sweet shop, the newsagents and other traders.

*John Drabble in the garden of 36 Meadow Bank Avenue*

The Drabble children did not mix a great deal with other Meadow Bank Avenue children. We know this from former residents' recollections as well as from Margaret's own account, but in a letter written to an Avenue resident in 1996 she wrote of, 'vivid recollections of proudly pushing baby brother Richard around the Avenue in his pram'. Mrs Drabble did not appear to engage in socialising with neighbours. She made an exception, however, for the family at number 38, the Smiths. They were friendly, kind people and Mrs Drabble coached their son in preparation for the Cambridge Entrance Exam.

Marie played little with her own children, encouraging them to focus on more scholarly activity and introducing them to the classics from an early age. There was always the expectation that the four children would follow their parents to Cambridge and this expectation was met by each one in turn. The three daughters all followed their mother's choice of subject, English. Richard, like his father, read Law.

Their mother's sister, Phyllis, frequently came to stay at Meadow Bank Avenue and she seems to have been more relaxed with her nieces and nephew. Phyllis introduced them to board games, cards and jigsaws. Margaret has written in The Pattern in the Carpet about her lifelong enjoyment of jigsaws, generated by these visits. In her novel The Peppered Moth, Margaret tells the story of Bessie Bawtry and four generations of her family. There are clear parallels with her own family: Bessie's life echoes her mother's and aunt Dora in the book (Bessie's sister) is based on Phyllis:

*'Dora, unlike Bessie, liked children, and enjoyed playing board games and card games and doing jigsaws with them. She taught them how to do French knitting with a cotton bobbin and nails, and how to make fluffy pom-poms from cardboard milk-bottle tops and the wool of unravelled jerseys. She helped them to make Christmas decorations out of silver paper, and dye an Easter egg with onion skin...She was a good auntie, and she smelled sweetly, of baby powder, perspiration and yellowy butter'.*

The girls had a love of nature and, like many children growing up in that era, spent time roaming freely and exploring 'wild places'. For Margaret Drabble, post-war overgrown gardens, the grounds of Kenwood House and Endcliffe Park were favourite haunts for exploring the undergrowth, catching tadpoles, minnows and sticklebacks. The family would enjoy picnics in the Peak District but they did not travel much, except to take holidays on the east coast at places like Filey and Mablethorpe, or visit family. Margaret was a teenager before she first visited London; she was taken there by her aunt Phyllis.

## Schooling

Susan and Margaret were accepted by Sheffield High School. Sadly Margaret did not like it; she had been happier at the local primary school in Pontefract during the family's evacuation period in the War. Both girls wrote about their early lack of confidence at school, but it is clear that the parents wanted all of their children to benefit from a good education, as they themselves had done. The girls usually walked to school and often spent time in the Botanical Gardens on their way home. They learnt to swim at Glossop Road baths and on Saturday mornings they would go to the Central Library.

All three daughters were later sent to the Mount School in York. This was a Quaker School where their mother had taught for a short time before her marriage. Both parents became Quakers after this (during the 1950s). Before that Marie had said she was an atheist and their Father had attended St Andrew's the local Anglican Church. Margaret had gone with him; she said that the experience led to a lasting dislike of organ music.

## A Darker Side

Clearly many of the references in the sisters' writings paint a positive picture of their life in Nether Edge: a loving father, a comfortable lifestyle, a natural world to explore and enjoy, a wealth of literature to plunder. Yet other references in their writings convey a very different picture, a much less happy image of the city, the neighbourhood and the childhood experienced there. The source of this ambivalence appears to be threefold: the family context in which they grew up, the times in which it took place, and their own sense of quality relative to the physical and cultural context in which they developed.

The dominant feature of what seems to have been a rather dysfunctional family was the mother. When she arrived in Meadow Bank Avenue Marie was superficially a successful and fortunate woman, well educated, married to a lawyer, and living in a large comfortable house with servant support. This apparent success however disguised a major frustration at what she felt had been a career derailed by the social protocols of the time. A glittering academic record full of potential had somehow morphed into a blind alley of provincial ordinariness. This frustration, intensified by a tendency to depression, possibly clinical, led to bitterness and anger, often taken out on husband and children.

Descriptions of her by her daughters, in articles and in thinly disguised characters in their novels, variously describe her as 'a manipulative woman', a 'terrible liar', a 'blood sucker and a shrew'. Her general attitude to children is described as dislike: 'children were noisy and quarrelsome', she was 'not kind to her children, and she screamed at invited friends'.

Living in such an environment was clearly stressful. The two older girls both lacked confidence; Margaret stammered as a young schoolgirl and has written openly about her recurrent bouts of depression. Susan spent long periods in bed suffering with severe asthma and struggled to build relationships. Their mother, 'felt and communicated extremes of nervous terror' creating a house which was a 'repository of so much grief'.

The family coped with this in different ways. The father withdrew and avoided confrontation, tolerating her idleness and tantrums and offering little support to the children, though they remained fond of him. AS Byatt says that she hid, physically and emotionally, surrounding herself in books, avoiding conversation until well into her teens. In a 1991 interview with the New York Times she admits that she didn't speak to anyone voluntarily until she was about 16. Margaret also found solace in books and, interestingly, in responding to the confrontational challenges that her critical mother put in front of her.

Of Richard and Helen's coping mechanisms we know little. Margaret has said that she and Susan were 'forever in their mother's gaze', but that 'Helen was good at evading her and Richard was much younger'. We can only speculate that they too found an outlet in their studies and academic successes.

All, including the mother, seemed intent on escape. John Drabble's novel, 'Scawsby', written after they had moved to Kent in 1954, talks of exchanging, 'the dark, dangerous works of Sheffield steel mills' for a 'land of clean, clear deserts'. And in 'The Peppered Moth' Margaret Drabble puts into the mouth of the mother figure a reflection that 'she was delighted to leave for good. She never went back. There was nobody there that she ever wished to see again'.

These family stresses were compounded by the times during which they lived on Meadow Bank Avenue, times dominated by the Second World War. It is true that they arrived on the Avenue well before war broke out and left well after it had ended. Clearly the years between 1939 and 1945 were traumatic for the family with father serving abroad and in obvious physical danger, children evacuated, rationing in place and air raids. But the impact of the war, intense as it was, extended way beyond the immediate years of conflict. By the mid 1930s the possibility of War was an accepted fact which remorselessly evolved into expectation with the Spanish Civil War and the rise of Fascism. By 1938 Air Raid Precautions were in place and shelters being dug. It was even suggested by John Drabble that they be dug on the Avenue green.

So by the end of the war, there had been years of worry and stress. And this did not cease with the close of hostilities. The consequences and sacrifices continued well into the 1950s. These were felt not just vicariously but directly in Sheffield and Nether Edge, physically in the lingering evidence of shelters and bomb damage and emotionally in the awareness of those not returning or returning as changed people: *'A grim cold, rationed land'.*

AS Byatt especially articulates the worries these extended years of wartime caused. In 'Ragnarok' she juxtaposes recollections of her childhood life in the shadow of wartime with a fascination for the Norse myths, finding an easy parallel between horrors of the two worlds, one fantastic and one real, dreaming again and again of Germans secreted under her metal bedstead, or crouched under benches and tea tables waiting to pounce, knowing that if they came the world would end.

Add to this a growing realisation of their intellectual and aesthetic sensibilities, which contrasted starkly with their perception of the physical and cultural environment of Sheffield. Physically the war left its mark, but on a landscape that was already blighted. Sheffield and the immediate area are variously described as *'sombre and silent'*, a *'debased and despoiled landscape'* containing *'decay and fermentation'* set amid *'vast, dark, soot-blackened mansions'.*

Culturally too this was a place *'not best known for its natural beauty or its artistic discrimination'.* Margaret Drabble perhaps encapsulates this growing disconnect best in 'The Pattern in the Carpet' when she recounts her revelation when, aged 17, she visits Italy and its Renaissance sights for the first time; *'How could such things be?'* she asks *'in a world that also gave birth to Nether Edge'.*

It is little wonder then that the sisters were so ambivalent about their time in Nether Edge. The attractions of a natural environment, idyllic childhood activities and a loving father on the one hand, and on the other, a torrid home life, lived in the context of a bleak social, cultural and physical scenario.

# HARRY HEAP, 'KING OF CARTOONISTS'
## John Austin

Anyone interested in sport and living in Sheffield during the 1940s to 1960s will surely recognise the name of Harry Heap. For almost 40 years he supplied the Star Group with over 10,000 cartoons documenting the trials and triumphs of the local sporting clubs as well as theatrical stars and political notables. In the process Heap became an integral part of Sheffield cultural life, though by birth he was Lancastrian. Born in Burnley at the turn

of the century Harry moved to Sheffield in his twenties to work on the local paper as a cartoonist, living on Meadowbank Avenue in Nether Edge for most of his life until he died in 1968.

His most famous achievements were the storyboards he produced for the Friday evening Star and the Saturday Green'Un ( so called because it was printed on green paper). These were remarkable displays of his talents combining striking drawings, quick wit and speed of work. The Saturday productions in particular required prodigious skills. The story boards would describe the events of the games as they unfolded, in cartoon and text, with the last drawings timed for 2 minutes before the end of the game. The completed storyboard would then appear in the Green Un that evening around an hour after the game. Concise, witty and sparkling these were, for many people, as great an attraction as the game accounts.

A frequent character in these cartoons was Alf, a pipe smoking, flat capped, down to earth, opinionated character who passed comment on events from 1938, a character Heap claimed was his own personification.

*Heap cartoon of Ozzie Owl and Bertie Blade reading the Green 'Un with 'Alf' looking on.*

Heap never achieved a national profile though a cartoon of Hitler safely surveying the front line from a deep, deep bunker, done during Heap's service in the War, was run in a number of national papers. Nor would he have been recognised other than through his drawings. His was a medium of the common man. Nevertheless, the plebeian nature of his output disguised a most accomplished artist. Heap had studied at Burnley Art College and taught at Sheffield College of Art. A reminder that good art need not be culturally rarified. Sadly no memoirs or reminiscences seem to have been left. What cultural gold dust if Alf had thought to comment on life in Nether Edge.

---

# MAURICE WILKINSON, ACTOR
## Louise Lecutier

Maurice Wilkinson was born in 1921. He is a native of Nether Edge and, apart from his Second World War service in the R.A.F., has always lived here. Now in his 97th year he has led a varied life, being at various times an actor, dancer, hotelier, chef and horologist. His father was born in Violet Bank Road but, by the time Maurice was born, his parents were living in Albany Road. They were married in 1919 at St. Andrew's Church and Maurice was their only child. He attended this church until it was demolished in 2000 and then joined the flock at the Cathedral. Maurice recalls that he wound up the clock every week at St. Andrew's for many years; climbing the 50 steps to do so. Such was his affection for St. Andrew's that he paid for the repairs and refurbishment of the clock whose face was painted in 'Saxon Blue'. He recalls that it was made by Potts of Leeds and after the church's demolition it was bought by someone in Bath.

His education began at Miss Cawood's Infant school at no. 35, Crescent Road and he then progressed to Miss Young's school at the top of Adelaide Road. That house was demolished in the 1980s, to be replaced by five detached houses. Maurice's lifelong love of railway travel started in 1932, when he began travelling by train to attend Dronfield Grammar School. He caught the train from Heeley Station. As a teenager he used to take his two Airedale dogs, Jean and Judy, on the train into the Peak District for their regular rambles. In the 1930s Maurice and his parents took a Thomas Cook holiday to Germany. Though it was the time that the Nazi jackboot had become evident, they were still allowed to travel to Germany. Maurice recalled that their party was stopped at the border by some rather intimidating officials in uniform, who searched the luggage of the entire group, suspecting English spies. For some unknown reason, his family's luggage was not searched but Maurice said that they all felt that they were not trusted by the locals. Since adulthood he has travelled all over Europe and Britain by train.

In 1939, at the start of the War, Maurice joined the R.A.F. He didn't want to fly, maintaining that, as he didn't have wings, he preferred staying on terra firma. Instead he was a clerk at different bases around the country. During this time the Wilkinson family moved to what is now his present home, just off Montgomery Road. Maurice was home on leave when Sheffield was bombed in the blitz of December 1940. He had been out but returned home when the bombing began; Maurice, his parents, two dogs, a cat and a canary, sheltered in the cellar. The house was hit by an incendiary bomb and he helped his father extinguish the fire with buckets of water over a two hour period. He still has the tail fin of the incendiary device, kept as a souvenir.

It was at these premises that they opened 'The Southlands Hotel', catering primarily for 'commercial travellers' and also people working in the theatre. After the War he helped his parents run the hotel, sometimes working as the chef. It was lit by gas light with gas mantles in every room. Even today there is still some gas lighting in the house, though in a nod to modernity, this is now aided by electricity. Maurice took over the hotel completely on the death of his parents. It was around this time, that he bought copies of the theatrical magazine, 'The Stage' in which he saw an advertisement for auditions being held for 'The Song of Norway', a musical based on the life of composer, Edvard Grieg.

As he had had elocution lessons from Audrey Hodgson, who lived at 52 Montgomery Road, Maurice thought he would have a go at the audition. He was successful and after appearing on stage in Drury Lane, in London's West End, he travelled the country with the touring production. He appeared in other musicals, including 'Brigadoon', in which he also danced, employing staff to run the hotel during these absences. In between acting and dancing in shows, during the actor's 'resting' period, he would sign on at the Labour Exchange. So regularly was he attending there that the staff offered him a job with them and so Maurice spent his remaining working years finding jobs for other people.

He finally closed the hotel when he was seventy, to enjoy a well earned rest and to recall the interesting and varied events of his long life. Other interests have included support for the re-establishment of the Peak Railway. He is remembered by other volunteers there for his involvement and in fundraising, when he collected newspapers, some of which came from his friend, Miss Connie Chipchase who lived on Crescent Road.

**Editor's note:**

The movement and clock face of the St Andrew's clock mentioned in this article are now part of 'A Dorset Collection of Clocks' at the Millhouse Cider Museum, Dorchester. A plaque commemorates the donation of the clock and church bells by the wife and three sons of William Alexander Tyzack in August 1892 (see the chapter on the Tyzack family.)

---

# ELAINE GARRARD, THEATRICAL PROPS MAKER

## Liz Jolley

The last director of The Sheffield Playhouse, Colin George, first employed Elaine Garrard when she won an Arts Council Bursary in 1967. Regarded as a 'genius' by George and his colleagues, she went with him to the Crucible when it opened in 1971.

Born in Edgware Middlesex, Elaine trained as a designer under Ralph Koltai at The Central School of Art in London and went on to assist Tanya Moiseiwitsch - the designer chiefly responsible for the now acclaimed Crucible auditorium. Moving to Sheffield she lived on Kenbourne Road, Nether Edge and eventually had her own home on Sandford Grove Road.

*Elaine Garrard with friend Chris Taylor 2004*

Turning her skills to prop and costume making, Elaine became freelance in 1977. She designed and produced for theatre productions in Sheffield, at Manchester Royal Exchange, for Alan

Ayckbourn's Theatre in The Round in Scarborough and for numerous shows in London's West End.

Elaine worked with Sheffield based Roger Glossop and Charlotte Scott on several visitor attractions and by the time of her death in 2008 her work in The Lake District had been seen by 2.5 million people! She co-designed "The World of Beatrix Potter" at Bowness on Windermere and when Renee Zellweger was filming "Miss Potter" in the Lake District, it was one of Elaine's models that she was presented with. She brought meticulous authenticity to all her work and because Beatrix Potter painted in watercolour on white paper, she made her models white and 'furred them up' using a similar approach.

A great animal lover, Elaine shared her home with innumerable cats, as well as a rescued lurcher named "Dog". She loved dog walking around Nether Edge, particularly Chelsea Park and 'the woods', finding interest and beauty in all she saw - whether it was the cow parsley in May, the birdsong, or finding just the right piece of wood to make the fool's stick for a production of King Lear!

Elaine had an allotment on Brincliffe Edge. Here, she created a tranquil space where she enjoyed spending days during a short illness before dying aged 63 in 2008.

---

# JUDITH SILVESTER, DANCE TEACHER
# Chris Venables

Judy Silvester's parents, Constance Grant and her husband Harry Silvester started the Constance Grant Dance Centre on Psalter Lane over 80 years ago. Their daughter, Miss Judy, born in 1937, was a dancer all her life, taught first by her mother, then at the Bush Davies Theatre College in London and the Lehmiski School of Ballet, Birmingham.

In 1949, when only 12 years old she was principal dancer in a show at the Tower Ballroom in Blackpool, where she performed for four summer seasons. One of her first jobs at the age of 17 meant taking part in seven different shows a week as a redcoat at Butlin's holiday camp in Filey. On completion of her training, she performed as a dancer and singer in cabaret and professional theatre. In her 20s, with dance partner Paul Beeton, she took the title of British Dance Exhibition Champion for three consecutive years.

Known to everyone as "Miss Judy", Judith took over the Constance Grant Dance Centre on Psalter Lane from her mother in the 1960s and for the following 50 years she trained thousands of pupils, many of whom went on to become stars in their own right. As the school expanded to nearly 700 pupils, she inspired generations of Sheffield youngsters, from tots to adults, and oversaw their regular shows at Sheffield City Hall as they played to sell-out audiences. Sally Baxendale remembers as a seven-year-old appearing as a penguin in Constance Grant's 1956 show at the Empire Theatre on Charles Street. Both Sally's daughter and granddaughter followed her as Constance Grant pupils. When chair of the Miss Dance of Great Britain organising committee Judy brought the prestigious event to Sheffield where it stayed until it outgrew the City Hall.

Judy was actively involved with local theatre companies including Teacher Operatics, Harlequins, Roses and Denys Edwards Players. But her key role was as director and choreographer of the Croft House Theatre Company, with which she worked for over 50 years. Friends said: *"Her commitment and passion were legendary and she became an inspiration to us all... She was able to move with ease from the highest level of professional dance training to gently coaching those less able to deliver a performance, with confidence and aplomb."* As an internationally respected dance teacher she enjoyed her time with the international association and was its president in 1992. Having achieved the highest qualifications in all genres of theatre and ballroom dancing, she coached, examined, directed and choreographed around the world. In her later life she lived in the coach house on Kingfield Road.

She died in Cyprus at the age of 75 when working as senior examiner with the International Dance Teachers' Association. Her daughters Karen Siddall and Tracey Southern succeeded her at The Constance Grant Dance Centre. Colleagues said that behind all the glitz and the glamour which was a big part of Judy's life, she was an ordinary fun-loving girl... a good cook and a brilliant host who loved her family and adored her grandchildren.

Source: Sheffield Telegraph obituary 9 July 2013.

# Part 2

# In Business

# THE TYZACK FAMILY, INDUSTRIALISTS

# Nick Waite

We all go back a long way, but the Tyzacks more than most. According to Don Tyzack's "Glass Tools and Tyzacks" ( www.tyzack.net) the unusual family name derives from the group of glassmakers who arrived from Lorraine in eastern France from the late 16th century. Lorraine had been a glassmaking centre for centuries, but a combination of declining trade and persecution of their new-found Protestant faith drove them to emigrate, many of them to England. Some scattered and changed occupations; at the end of the 18th century, their descendant John Tyzack was the tenant of a farm on Trap Lane, which runs from Bents Green down towards the Porter Brook and Whitely Wood Hall. Two of his sons, Thomas (1789-1864) and William(1) (1782-1858) formed a partnership as manufacturers of saws, scythes and other edge tools. (Too many Tyzacks were called William; for clarity I have called three of William(1)'s descendants who inherited his business Williams 2, 3 and 4).

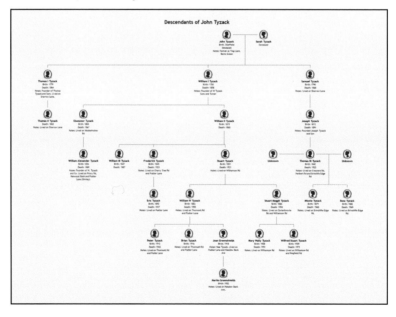

The Sheffield Tyzacks were extraordinarily energetic and successful business people: during the 19th century, John's descendants created six manufacturing businesses, four of them in direct competition with a similar range of products.

After his partnership with William ended, Thomas became the first of the family to live in or near Nether Edge, trading as Thomas Tyzack and Sons from a substantial house and land on Sharrow Lane and from Walk Mill on the Limb Brook, a tributary of the Sheaf. However both Thomas and his son, another Thomas, died within a year of each other, in 1865 and

*Little London Works.*

1866, and very quickly, the partnership of two of the surviving sons was dissolved. Individually they carried on in the same trade for a few years , but appear to have transferred the right to the name Thomas Tyzack and Sons to a Glaswegian businessman who himself got into financial difficulties in 1871. A sad ending for the first Tyzack business connected to Nether Edge.

Then between 1880 and 1890 the competing cousins of three of the other family tool companies came to live nearer the centre of Nether Edge; we concentrate first on the business founded by William (1), W Tyzack Sons and Turner, because the firm's most substantial factory was built on the edge of our area - and because the very last Nether Edge Tyzack was his three times great granddaughter. Why 'and Turner'? William (1) had three sons – William (2), Ebenezer and Joshua, who all joined the business, together with his son in law Benjamin Turner; in fact Benjamin's great grandson Norman Turner was a Director when the company became a PLC in the modern era.

In 1825 William(1) took a lease of substantial land in Rockingham Street, but the development of the business is a good example of a Sheffield pattern of production in small units along the river valleys to the West of the city. Today it is difficult to imagine how many mills and water wheels once lined the Porter and Sheaf, many of them of mediaeval origin; no less than 20 such sites have been identified on the Porter and its tributaries and 30 on or near the Sheaf.

The productive capacity at Rockingham Street was soon inadequate, and in 1831 William(1), became the tenant of the Whirlow Wheel on the Limb Brook (very near to his brother Thomas' Walk Mill) but by 1847 this too was inadequate and he took a tenancy of Whiteley Wood Works from a descendant of Thomas Boulsover, the owner of the Hall and the inventor of old Sheffield Plate. These works were adjacent to the Porter, and near to his father's farm; the works were certainly substantial and comprised what were called the Emery Wheel, the Saw Wheel and the Cutlery Wheel.

*The Tilt Forge at Little London Works, 1975. Photo, P.Machan*

Still needing greater capacity, in 1849 William(1) became a significant figure in Sheffield's industrial history by acquiring the tenancy of the Abbeydale Works on the Sheaf owned by the Fitzwilliam Estate. This tenancy continued until 1935, long after the business relied on water power, and the site was then purchased by Alderman Graves and given to the city and is the basis of the Abbeydale Industrial Hamlet. The substantial working facilities also included a manager's house and for many years the Census returns show that William(1) and two generations of his successors were either brought up or spent their family lives in the cramped accommodation, which can still be inspected. Now the family business concentrated entirely on expansion within the Sheaf valley; from the 1850s to the 1870s, the firm either bought or took tenancies of Totley Rolling Mills, the Totley Forge, Old Hay Wheel and the Smithy Wood Tilt. Then the final piece of the jigsaw fell into place with the acquisition in 1876 of Heeley Corn Mill near to Little London Dam, with a large area of vacant land adjacent to the Midland railway. Water power was being replaced with modern machinery, and the business HQ was moved from Rockingham Street to the industrial complex created on a 12 acre site between Little London Road and what is now Broadfield Road.

*The File workshops at Little London Works, 1975. Photo, P. Machan.*

William(2) succeeded his father but continued to live at Abbeydale, where he had four sons including Frederick (1849-1923), William(3) (1847-1887) and Stuart (1851-1921). It was Frederick and Stuart whose growing families, wealth and status led them to follow their great uncle Thomas to large and respectable homes in the developing suburb of Nether Edge, but

they were not the first. After their uncle Ebenezer died in 1867, there were too many male Tyzacks to be fitted into William Tyzack Sons and Turner, and Ebenezer's son William Alexander founded W A Tyzack and Co in direct competition with his cousins, both in their product range and in the grandeur of the houses they created for themselves in the new suburb. Ebenezer and William Alexander migrated into Nether Edge by stages. In 1841 Ebenezer lived in Ecclesall Road and later moved to Washington Road and then to a Priory Villa on Wostenholm Road. William Alexander lived at 17 Priory Road after he married and later on Kenwood Bank, but then purchased a large block of land from the Newboulds, on which he created a substantial estate on the corner of Psalter Lane and Cherry Tree Road, directly opposite to the Newbould family's own Sharrow Bank. (See Shelagh Woolliscroft's article in this book.)

Frederick, Stuart and Stuart's sons William(4) and Stuart Meggitt Tyzack all settled in Nether Edge a few years later, first in relatively modest houses before building, inheriting or purchasing something more suited to their wealth and status. Frederick lived at Abbeydale until after the 1881 Census, by 1891 he was living on Cherry Tree Road and by 1901 at Psalter House on a large corner site between Psalter Lane, Kingfield Road and Brincliffe Crescent, with the postal address of 127 Psalter Lane. (Psalter House was later demolished and is now the site of the Kingfield Centre of the Orthodox Synagogue Sheffield and an adjoining block of flats intended for elderly members of the community).

Frederick became Chairman of the family business in 1906; his elder brother William(3) had died unmarried and childless in 1887, never having left the Abbeydale base of work and home. Frederick remained in post until his death in 1923 but there the male line was temporarily broken; Frederick's only son, Eric D Tyzack joined the fledgling Royal Flying Corps in the Great War and was shot down and killed over Passchendaele in 1917.

Meanwhile, about 1890 Frederick's brother Stuart Tyzack had purchased a large plot of land near St Andrews Church where he created the house at 7 Williamson Road which he and his younger son and his grandchildren occupied successively for just over 100 years. Stuart had two sons, William

**Colonel Wilfred Stuart Tyzack**

(4) (1883-1955) and Stuart Meggitt Tyzack (1886-1954). Ordinarily William(4) as the elder son would inherit Williamson Road after Stuart's death in 1921 but by then he had made his own more impressive move. The younger brother Stuart Meggitt Tyzack had been working in France on European sales for the Company, where he had married the German Auguste Meizer and their two children Mary Wally Tyzack (1908-1991) and Wilfred Stuart Tyzack (1909-1973) were born. However by 1911 they were back in Sheffield and living at 244 Carterknowle Road, not actually in Nether Edge but even more convenient for the Abbeydale base and the now very substantial Little London Works. After his father's death he and his young family moved into Williamson Road, where his daughter Mary lived until her death in 1991, the subject of another chapter in this book.

After his marriage, William(4) lived at 9 Thornsett Road until 1919, when he purchased the last and perhaps the grandest of the Tyzack mansions in Nether Edge, the former home of the Newboulds known as Sharrow Bank; this part of the story is included in the article on the house and its three notable families. In due course William(4) and his family moved to Fulwood, leaving only their Williamson Road cousins as Nether Edge Tyzacks, with one exception; on her marriage to Hugh Greenshields his daughter Joan moved to a house on Meadow Bank Avenue where they were neighbours of my growing family until 1974.

Mary and Wilfred were only 28 and 27 when their cousins left Sharrow Bank. Neither was yet married, indeed Mary never was, and Wilfred still had to experience his "good war" after which he always appears in directories as Colonel Wilfred S Tyzack MC TD; he made a late marriage in 1952, had no children of his own, and became Chairman of W Tyzack Sons and Turner in 1961. After his marriage, he and his wife and stepchildren moved to the last house built on Elizabeth Newbould's Kingfield Estate, a fine detached property at 78 Kingfield Road, originally the home of R J Stokes, whose company manufactured paints in a factory on Little London Road. This was very near to the Tyzack factory complex – another example of businessmen in the Sheaf valley looking to Nether Edge as a convenient home in pleasant middle class society.

Stuart Meggitt Tyzack died in 1954, his wife Auguste in 1960 and their son Wilfred in 1973. That left only Mary, still in grand if eccentric splendour at 7 Williamson Road, rightly remembered as one of our great Nether Edge characters.

An appeal for any other evidence of Tyzack residents of Nether Edge produced a surprise; both 62 and 64 Brincliffe Edge Road had been in the ownership of a Thomas Tyzack and two of his children. They had moved into No 62 in 1911 from elsewhere in Nether Edge; and both properties remained in the family's ownership until after the 1939-45 War. This Thomas Tyzack (1842-1923) had assumed management and then ownership of Joseph Tyzack and Son after his father Joseph retired. Joseph (1813-1891) was born on Dobbin Hill in Ecclesall, a grandson of the farmers John and Sarah Tyzack from Trap Lane in Bents Green. Joseph specialised in tools for builders and he devised and patented the plasterer's steel float for smoothing newly applied plaster on domestic and other walls, a tool universally employed to this day.

Like Ebenezer and William Alexander, Joseph and his family moved to Nether Edge by stages. In 1851 they were living in New George Street in the city centre, but by 1861 they were in Fitzwilliam Street next to or within their works premises, much like the Tyzacks in the manager's house at Abbeydale. Over the next 20 years Thomas married and had three daughters and two sons; by 1871 the young family were living on Wilson Road, near Hunters Bar. Then in 1876, Thomas built the extensive Meersbrook Works in Valley Road Heeley - coincidentally the same year as W Tyzack Sons and Turner bought the Heeley Corn Mill which became the basis of Little London Works.

*Captain Peter Tyzack*
*(killed in action in Sicily 1943)*

Like Frederick, Stuart and William Alexander, Nether Edge must have seemed to Thomas a good place to settle and raise their families – near their works, a developing and safe middle class suburb, with many houses adequate to their needs and with accommodation for their servants. By 1901 Thomas and his family were living at 39 Crescent Road and later they moved to 1 Herbert Road, from where Thomas bought 62 and 64 Brincliffe Edge Road in 1911. Now a widower, he was living with his unmarried daughters Minnie and Rosanna or Rose; their

*Tyzack Trade Advertisements*

address is given in Whites 1912 Directory as No 62 and after Thomas' death in 1923 Minnie and Rose continued to live there until 1931 or 1932. About that time (though the family retained both 62 and 64 as investments until 1946), the sisters moved from Nether Edge to 16 Harley Road, newly built on Fitzwilliam land. There they lived together, unmarried and childless, until Rose died in 1969 and Minnie in 1970. The sisters' long lives, cushioned by wealth and comfort, seem unremarkable - except for one startling fact. After Thomas's retirement, Joseph Tyzack and Son was managed by his son Clement who died young in 1918 and was succeeded by Minnie and Rose. Then aged 39 and 36, they were presumably advised and supported by their father until his death in 1923; even today that might be unusual in a substantial manufacturing company but in the 1920s it was remarkable. I have unearthed no other personal details, but they must have been formidable ladies, and were still recorded as joint Managing Directors in a 1939 Directory in the National Archives, shortly before the firm first became part of a larger group in 1942/3.

So many Tyzacks came to live in Nether Edge because the developing suburb was ideal for those who could buy or create homes to reflect their status, success and hard work - particularly in the cases of the owners of W Tyzack Sons and Turner and Joseph Tyzack and Son, as their resources derived from a chain of productive sites and industrial complexes strung along the nearby Sheaf valley.

How long did they choose to stay here?  With increasing personal mobility in the age of the car, a new pattern emerged; a move further to the west of the city into newer and more salubrious suburbs.   William Alexander's descendants had moved to Dore by the 1920s, William (4) to Fulwood in 1936 and then in retirement to Wiltshire; Minnie and Rose migrated to Ecclesall.  Only Stuart Meggit Tyzack's children Mary and Wilfred stayed in the area, only 7 Williamson Road remained in Tyzack family ownership until nearly the end of the last century.

And the businesses which they had established and provided their wealth? With hindsight it is difficult to imagine the independence of any of their companies continuing untroubled by the rise of foreign competition, government policies, and the wave of amalgamations and takeovers – the three factors which contributed to the decimation of so much of Sheffield's traditional industries.

William(4) had died in 1955; his elder son Brian took little or no part in management of W Tyzack Sons and Turner and crucially, the younger son Peter (who was expected to do so) was killed in Sicily in 1943 attacking a German machine gun post.  Like Frederick's son Eric, killed in 1917, who knows what their survival might have meant to the continuing management of their family company? In fact neither W Tyzack Sons and Turner or W A Tyzack and Co survived; the final irony was that in 1987 the business of W Tyzack Sons and Turner was absorbed in W A Tyzack and Co.  Little London Works were demolished in 1988, and the site now houses a gym, a pub, the local HQ of a national accountancy firm and other office and retail uses. Similarly only the façade of Joseph Tyzack and Son's Meersbrook Works remains on Valley Road. This is typical of what has happened to so much of Sheffield's manufacturing history; having given employment to very many residents of Sharrow, Nether Edge, Heeley and Meersbrook  the thriving industrial complexes of Little London and Meersbrook Works are now only a memory to older residents. There was a management buyout of the amalgamated Tyzack companies in 1989 but the combined enterprise did not last long, going into receivership in 1991.

The experience of Joseph Tyzack and Son was rather different. Starting in in the early years of WW2, the company which Minnie and Rose had managed for over 20 years entered into a sequence of amalgamations, and was finally absorbed into Spear and Jackson plc in the 1970s, where it exists today as a highly respected brand and a range of plastering tools and builders' trowels in their current catalogue, together with the original 3 legged logo dating from the founder Joseph Tyzack's strong trading relationship with the Isle of Man. With only this exception the name Tyzack has disappeared as completely from the business world as from the roster of Nether Edge residents.

See also Shelagh Woolliscroft's article on Shirley in this book.

**Sources:**

www.tyzack.net *'Glass Tools and Tyzacks'*
www.riversheaf.org.uk   trowelcollectorblogspot.co.uk
*'They Lived in Sharrow and Nether Edge'* NENG History Group 1988

With thanks to; Martin Greenshields, Nick and Anne Hutton, Helen McDonald, Richard Pethen, Chris Venables, Steve Burgin and the family's own historian Don Tyzack.

---

# THOMAS & ALICE ROBERTS, RETAILERS

## Penny Burnham

Many people will remember the Roberts Brothers department store, which used to stand on the Moor. The leading members of the Roberts family lived in Nether Edge, but the fact that they were both family and neighbours didn't mean they got on with each other, and in the end there were two Roberts's stores, one more successful than the other.

*Looking up the Moor towards Pinstone Street in the 1890s; T&J Roberts store on the left*

The firm of T & J Roberts, wholesale and retail drapers and house furnishers was started by

Thomas Roberts on the Moor in 1859 and his brother John joined him three years later. T & J Roberts was so successful that in 1881 they built extensive premises at Moorhead, opposite the Crimean War Monument.

John Roberts lived at 35 Kenwood Park Road with his wife Mary Ellen (Sharman), and Thomas and his

*Brantwood*

wife Alice lived not far away at Brampton Villa, a detached house at 23 Montgomery Road. But in 1891 John died. His widow Mary Ellen did not get on with Thomas's wife Alice and so she gave two of her sons, Charles and J Arnold, £1000 to start a rival drapers business. This new firm was called Roberts Brothers and had its main shop on the Moor. In due course Charles married and went to live at Hathersage but Arnold remained at Kenwood Park Road with Mary Ellen and his siblings.

At the time of John's death, Thomas and his wife Alice were still living on Montgomery Road with their three sons, William Arthur, Thomas Harland, and Edward Lamplugh. But Thomas snr. had bigger plans, and designed Brantwood, 1 Kenwood Bank (now Brantwood Specialist School), a large house in a fairly traditional style which was already old-fashioned. But he died in 1893 well before the building was completed in 1899-1900. Thomas was a prominent Wesleyan and his funeral at the fashionable Brunswick Chapel at the bottom of the Moor, where he had long been Circuit chairman, attracted over 800 attendees including a large number of Wesleyan ministers.

Alice never moved in to the new house, but sectioned off the far side of the land on Kenwood Bank and built her own style of house on it. This house 3 Kenwood Bank is in the Arts & Craft style and cost her £5,000 to build, which was a great deal of money then. When she died in 1926 the house only sold for £1,600. It is not only of modern design for the time, but of very modern construction with a concrete float base (so no cellars) and a steel girder frame. She broke the Wolstenholme Estate building covenants by not building in stone, but rather used bricks, so was compelled to render the whole house, which is why it is the only white, non-stone-fronted house in the area. In the "New & Altered Property Register" for buildings needing to be Rateable-Valued, 3 is not listed in the September 1900 entry but it is

*3 Kenwood Bank*

listed in the March 1901 entry so we can assume that it was completed in the winter of 1900/1901.

At about the same time Thomas and Alice's son Thomas Harland Roberts, who became head of T & J Roberts after his father's death, built 50 Kenwood Road, at the corner of Cherrytree Road. This house was also very modern for the time with imitation half-timbering anticipating the suburban architecture of the interwar period.

The original business T & J Roberts did not survive the Slump and went into liquidation in the 1930s, but Roberts Bros. continued on the Moor until they were bombed on December 12/13 1940. T & J Roberts' empty Moorhead building was now owned by the Council, and was used to store coffins during the War.  Arnold Roberts, needing premises to continue his business, approached the Sheffield City Council and rented the premises until a new building was erected after the war. They also had shops at Ecclesall Rd and London Rd. The new shop on the Moor opened in 1954.  Roberts Brother merged with Eyres in 1982, and the Roberts family sold their interest in 1984. The site has now been redeveloped and 'The Light' cinema now stands here.

*Roberts Brothers on the Moor, 1970s.*

# WILLIAM BRAGGE & SHIRLE HILL

## Pril Rishbeth

The Shirle Hill that we see today was not the same as the house that William Bragge bought from John Brown in 1865. Despite William being the owner for only 12 years (1865-77), with the help of architects Firth Bros and Jenkinson, he transformed Brown's modest Georgian house into an impressive Victorian Italianate building. A similar project had been carried out on a larger scale by Prince Albert for the Royal family at Osborne House on the Isle of Wight.

*William Bragge's Shirle Hill*

The original Shirle Hill house was re-fronted to compliment the large Italianate extension, complete with tower. Pevsner later described the house "as an odd mixture of rendered elevations, stone lintel and rusticated giant pilasters which terminate in elaborate finials on the older part. A tall Italianate tower to the rear". The whole would house Bragge's growing family, his collections and reflect his position. He was to become Master Cutler in 1870.

William Bragge was a man of the Victorian Age. He embodied the enquiring mind and far-reaching interests of his time. Born the son of a Birmingham jeweller, he studied mechanics and mathematics in Birmingham and trained as an engineer and surveyor. He was a surveyor on the Chester to Holyhead railway line before going out to Brazil. In Rio de Janeiro he helped install gas and electricity and surveyed for the first railway line in

*Shirle Hill in 2018*

Brazil. His railway interest presumably inspired him to name his second son, born there, George Stephenson Bragge. The Emperor Dom Pedro II awarded him the Order of the Rose, (the ribbon for which is held in the Sheffield archives), in appreciation of his work. In fact Bragge and Dom Pedro shared so many interests that it is suggested that when the Emperor (called The Magnanimous), was travelling incognito in Europe in 1871 he visited Bragge at Shirle Hill.

From Brazil, Bragge moved to Sheffield to work for John Brown at his Atlas Steel works, and was made a Managing Director. He was involved in establishing the armour plate manufactory. Leaving Sheffield in 1872, he went to Paris. Here things didn't go so well for him. His one failure was attempting a sewage system for the Societe des Engrais. He returned to England in 1876 and settled in his birth city of Birmingham, calling his house there Shirle Hill. Here his engineering took another turn, for he organised the successful manufacture of watches by machinery on the American system. Unfortunately before he died in 1884, he went blind.

William Bragge was an engineer of repute, but during his time in Sheffield he involved himself in many activities beyond his work at Atlas. He served on the Council, becoming a member of the Public Libraries committee, and as part of the Literature and Philosophical Society, he was able to influence the handing over of their museum collection to the library. This formed the nucleus for the setting up of the City Museum in Weston Park.

Bragge was the speaker at the School of Art in Surrey Street in 1874 and copies of his speech are held in the city archives. The speech is wide reaching, remarkable for its scope and even relevant today. Starting with the need to enlarge the School of Art, he went on to the need for better education for every child and suggesting the appointment of a Minister for Education. He argued that Europe was doing better and leaving Sheffield behind to face foreign competition. Every worker in the iron, silver and cutlery works should have access to a broad education and understand the whole process of production. He recommended setting up a Metal Work Museum. He pointed out the excellence of museums being set up at the time, namely in South Kensington but also in towns like Halifax, Huddersfield, Nottingham and Birmingham. Prince Albert had given a lead and Bragge was sure the V & A, and the British Museum would loan exhibits rather than keep items in cellars. He emphasised the need for Sheffield to move ahead or lose out to others.

But Bragge is perhaps best known as an antiquarian and bibliophile. He collected. His biggest collection was everything to do with smoking. He created a bibliography (Bibliotheca Nicotiana) of all books related to tobacco which he published and later revised. He also had a collection of artefacts such as pipes (13,000 of them!) types of tobacco and snuff boxes. He also collected all the works of Cervantes - 1,500 volumes which he donated to the Birmingham Free Library in 1873. Unfortunately these were all lost in the fire of 1879.

Somehow he found time to travel and learn languages. On his extensive travels in Europe, Russia, Egypt and America, he amassed assorted objects that interested him. A cabinet of gems and precious stones from all parts went to Birmingham Art Gallery. Other objects found their way to the British Museum.

*"Ye Great Bragge...from foreign parts with his curiosities"*

He didn't actually sell his Shirle Hill house in Sheffield until 1877 when the sale catalogue makes clear that the house was stuffed with books and curiosities. The New York Times of 11 June 1882, in a Gossipy Foreign news item, mentions the sale in London of some of Bragge's collections. This would have been when he was going blind. It is clear that, although he liked to be surrounded with many of his acquisitions, he was a great supporter of museums, art galleries and libraries.

This man of many parts was a Fellow of the Society of Antiquaries, the Anthropological Society, the Royal Geographical Society and many foreign societies. There were many remarkable men and women who embodied the spirit of the Victorian Age, and it seems that William Bragge should be included amongst them.

# WILLIAM HATFIELD, METALLURGIST

# Tom Heller

We are fortunate to be able to discover quite a lot about Dr W H Hatfield, F.R.S. (1882-1943), who lived in Brincliffe House from 1936 to 1943. Not only because his professional achievements have been well documented, but also because he wrote a very personal book spelling out his ideas, ideals and philosophy. The book is called 'Sheffield Burns'[1]. It was written in anger during the Second World War after he had observed the effects on Sheffield of the German bombing raids during December 1940 from the terrace of Brincliffe House.

*Between 3.30 and 4.0 a.m. on 13th December 1940, from our terrace (at Brincliffe House) we watched Sheffield burn. Sheffield is my native city. I felt then that the rest of my life must be devoted to helping to restore and rebuild the fortunes of the city which had its roots in Norman times and which had become that which it was by the work of many generations of earnest men (p.7 'Sheffield Burns').*

Since its construction in 1853 Brincliffe House, one of the grand houses that stand on Brincliffe Crescent, had been owned by a series of industrialists. Its grounds stretch back through an elegant driveway towards an gateway on Osborne Road. The house was designed to present an image of solidity and a certain gravitas rather than grandeur – suitable for people enjoying substantial wealth and a decent, rather than greatly elevated, position in society. Thus, a tobacco manufacturer, a brewer and an engineer had lived in Brincliffe House in turn before William H. Hatfield bought the property in 1936 when he was 52 years old. He was well established and, as we shall see, financially secure.

Until a few years ago the house was occupied by offices of the NHS but today it is being restored to residential use. Prior to the growth of the trees on

*Brincliffe House, Brincliffe Crescent.*

Brincliffe Crescent and the building of houses on the opposite side it is easy to imagine the spectacular and disturbing view that the Hatfields must have had from the terrace as they watched the city burn that night.

Hatfield's writing takes us on a somewhat rambling journey through his philosophy, politics and ideology. The book has been written almost in the style of a stream of consciousness. He spells out his views on a very wide range of subjects including patriotism, workers' rights, capitalism and foreign travel.

Hatfield died just four days after handing over the manuscript to his publishers. In a moving prelude to the book his wife Edith, writes

*He died on Sunday 17th October (1943), through strain and overwork in furthering our war effort, working unflinchingly at all hours day and night for four years without rest or holiday, for our armaments and aircraft industry* (p.5).

William Hatfield was a metallurgist who is best known for his work in the early development and refinement of specialist types of stainless steel. He was the son of Martha Sheppard and Francis Hatfield, the works manager of the world-famous cutlery manufacturer, Joseph Rodgers. Rather than following his father onto the shop floor, William's career focussed exclusively on analysis and research into industrial processes, mainly iron and steel manufacture. His study of analytical chemistry began as a student at

Sheffield Central Technical School in Leopold Street which led to his first job in the laboratory of Henry Bessemer & Co. This initial employment/ apprenticeship included the opportunity to study metallurgy

*Brown-Firth Research laboratories at the junction of Princess Street and Blackmore Street, Attercliffe. Purpose built in 1908 the building is now Grade II listed and recognised as the birthplace of stainless steel.*

during evening classes at University College (which became Sheffield University in 1905).

William was a capable student who was able to make good use of College facilities, particularly those associated with analytical techniques such as microscopy and thermal analysis. In 1902 he was awarded an 'Associateship' in Metallurgy along with the Mappin Medal for being the best college student of his year. His early career was marked by employment in a number of analytical laboratories while at the same time continuing his formal studies. He was awarded two further degrees in metallurgy before becoming one of the first Doctors of Metallurgy at Sheffield University in 1913.

It is clear that William lived in interesting, transitional times. The era in which he started his work was at the birth of a technical, industrial movement that put Sheffield at the centre of specialist steel production. Several of the educational opportunities that he was able to use so effectively have been lost or changed beyond recognition – the Central Technical School has now become a series of restaurants and wine bars in Leopold Square and, symbolically, his second place of work - the laboratories of J. Crowley and Company at Meadow Hall Ironworks - has since been razed to the ground and become part of the Meadowhall Retail Park.

By 1916 William Hatfield was a fully trained metallurgist and took over from Harry Brearley (the inventor of stainless steel), as head of Brown-Firth Research Laboratories. He remained in this post until his death in 1943. His investigative output was prodigious and he published a great number of original research papers that have led to the development of many of the specialised stainless and heat-resistant steels available to modern engineers and product developers.

It is no coincidence that Hatfield's career is book-ended by two World Wars, during which time there was intense pressure to produce special steel that could be used for improved arms manufacture in order to gain military advantage. The addition of 12.8% of chromium to steel was discovered initially by Brearley in the Brown Firth Research Laboratories to prevent rust and corrosion in rifle barrels and in the lining of large guns.  After Brearley left the company Hatfield was appointed head of research and he continued to develop innovative alloys of steel and explore their properties.   With the addition of a wide variety of different materials, such as nickel and carbon, to steel in various proportions he was able to create specialist steel alloys with particular properties such as improved creep resistance ("creep" is the phenomenon of a metal slowly deforming under low stresses at high temperatures, such as might occur in an engine).

In the inter-war period the development of high quality stainless steel for cutlery and other domestic items became important commercially.  Hatfield discovered that a modified composition of steel including 18% chromium and 8% nickel was ideal for forging, rolling, pressing, riveting and brazing into cutlery shapes that could then be highly polished.   This steel, known originally as 18/8, was patented and became known commercially as 'Firth Staybrite Silver Steel' with widespread, successful commercial applications. The addition of nickel to the iron-chromium alloy helped improve corrosion resistance under a wider range of conditions, and made the steel less brittle at low temperatures. Throughout the 1920s and 1930s steel research became increasingly focussed on the properties of steel required for specific domestic and military production. Hatfield was much in demand to give talks about his research work and the new types of steel that he had developed. He travelled widely throughout Europe, but it was America, and the productivity of the workers there, that particularly impressed him:

... 'Americans, who collectively were obviously buoyant, prosperous, happy and full of energy...the scale of production I found to be truly colossal' (p.184).

William Hatfield also visited Germany on a number of occasions and worked with research scientists at Krupp to develop and patent the special steels that were subsequently used by both sides in the Second World War. He read Mein Kampf in an attempt to understand the motivation for Germany's aggressive stance (p.30), and during one visit to Berlin in April 1939 he caught a fleeting glimpse of Hitler. He was less impressed by the German workers who he observed to be 'a people obviously downtrodden, broken-spirited and nearly without hope' (p.184).

**Politics and philosophy**

Hatfield's father was a Unitarian and his mother a member of the Church of England.  He describes his study of Epicurus and the Stoics but states that he 'finally fell into the hands of the Determinists' (p.28). Determinists believe that every event, decision and action is determined by previously existing factors. To be honest it is quite hard from Hatfield's writing to discern a consistent deterministic theme - except that he seemed largely content with the social order as he found it between the two World Wars. Perhaps these quotes give a taste of his views:

*'It is clear that a few outstanding people provide the means of making it possible for all men to use and enjoy the "fruits of the earth"* (p.35).

*Unskilled work will continue to require to be done, and the ideal State would appear to be the one in which each individual is occupied with the work for which he or she is best fitted* (p.70).

Perhaps because of his personal trajectory Hatfield was a strong believer in the benefits of education and he advocates at length for self-educated people who have ability *'... and they should certainly not have it continually rubbed into them that because their fathers could not afford to give them a public school education they are therefore for ever classed as inferior types of human beings'* (p.80). Perhaps he was revealing something of his own experiences as an ambitious and talented man from comparatively humble stock.

Hatfield's generosity when he was himself established didn't extend to the working classes whom he expected not to make demands for extra wages.

*I am afraid that it is not always appreciated by the workpeople that for every hour's work for which they are paid the organized business in which he is working must receive back from the ultimate market something in excess of the value of his efforts if employment is to be continuous.* (p.85)

So how was Hatfield, a waged research worker himself from a comparatively humble background, able to afford to buy and run Brincliffe House? In his book 'Sheffield Burns' (1943) he recounts a story:

*... (a friend) was staying with me and after dinner we were sitting having a quiet talk and smoke in my library. At one point in the conversation he said, "I like this place (Brincliffe House), I like your library, I like your garden, in fact I think it is all very delightful." I could not resist saying, "Yes! It is quite nice, isn't it, and you will be very interested to know that the whole place didn't cost me a penny." I explained that I had bought industrial shares in a number of companies, they had gone up in value, I had sold some of them and the difference in value had more than paid for the house and the land* (pp. 128-9).

So what sort of person was William Herbert Hatfield? His obituary in the Journal of the Institute of Mechanical Engineers describes him as

*… a great leader of young men, a delightful lecturer, a good companion, a generous citizen, a keen student of international affairs, and a practiced after-dinner speaker, only rarely making use of notes.  Those who were closely associated with him will always remember his dynamic energy, great enthusiasm and driving power, his quick appraising glance, his lightning summing up of a situation, and his rapier-like thrusts in debate.*

Phew!, it makes me quite tired just thinking about him.  We also know that he collected awards and honours throughout his career including the Bessemer Gold Medal of the Iron and Steel Institute and was elected to become a Fellow of the Royal Society in 1935.  He was the first president of the Sheffield Metallurgical Association (an organisation which he had previously founded), and served on many official government advisory committees during the Second World War.

He also loved to circulate in the upper echelons of society and in his book he recalls his meetings with Churchill, Mussolini, Lord Austin, Henry Ford, Lord Nuffield, Amy Johnson (who lived nearby in Sheffield), and a large number of other notables although I don't think any of them came to visit him in Brincliffe House.

To be honest little is recorded of his private life and no mention is made of family or domestic circumstances within the 213 pages of his book.  We know that he married Edith Marion Seagrave, a woman from Nottingham, in 1907, but she doesn't get a single mention in his book even though his obituary claims that 'the devoted companionship (of his wife) sustained him throughout the strenuous years of work and responsibility'. No children are recorded and Amy Johnson is the only woman who gets a mention in his writings. The census of 1939 shows that he shared Brincliffe House with three Ediths!  In addition to his wife, Edith Marion Hatfield there is an Edith Burgin and an Edith Bown. Presumably they were servants, living on the top floor of Brincliffe House, sustaining their master, providing him with the support needed to pursue his great works - but none thought worthy of mention or thanks in his book.

**Sources:**

Hatfield, Dr W H (1943) *Sheffield Burns.*  J.W.Northend Ltd. Sheffield.
Densch, C H (1944)  *William Herbert Hatfield: Biographical Memoir.*
Royal Society.

# WALLACE HEATON, Chemist's Assistant to Royal Photographer.                Kay Phillips

Wallace Heaton might not be a familiar name today but in the first half of the 20th century he was a very prominent figure in the field of photography. He and his family lived at 36 Meadow Bank Avenue from c1904-8, before moving to Grindleford and then London, but his obituaries record that he always held Sheffield in great affection and, 'looked back with pleasure on his years in Sheffield, appreciating the friendly atmosphere in the city'.... He said of London, 'You never get that neighbourly spirit down here'. Wallace Heaton's life is an interesting example of how astute business decisions could generate enormous personal and financial benefits, even during periods of national crisis or severe economic depression.

Wallace was born near Stockton-on-Tees, moving to Leyburn in North Yorkshire aged five, after the death of his Mother in 1884. He was an only child and when he left school Wallace served an apprenticeship in Lupton's chemist shop in York. He gradually progressed, completing his Minor exams at Manchester College of Pharmacy and Majors at the Metropolitan College. After working as a Chemist's Assistant in London and Chemist shop Manager in Brighton, he bought a shop of his own in Sheffield in 1902. He was 24 and the shop was The Angel Pharmacy known as Watson's on the High Street.

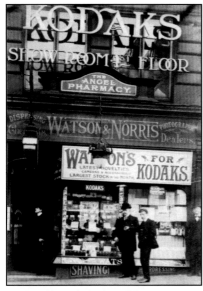

*Watson's Pharmacy, High Street, Sheffield.*

Wallace Heaton was in the right place at the right time and he seized the opportunity to grow his business and his fortune. Amateur photography was just beginning to become popular with a wider general public and chemists were the only people who could provide the chemicals for film processing. He expanded the chemist shop into a business supplying photographic materials and equipment to both amateurs and professionals. He also recognised the power of advertising and raised the profile of his business through eye-catching posters and advertisements. These were often in the style of humorous cartoons.

*Photograph of 36 Meadow Bank Avenue in 1906*

*Ethel and the children in the garden 1907*

Wallace married Ethel May Cundy in 1903. They lived at 36 Meadow Bank Avenue from 1904. The photograph shows the picture he took of Ethel with their daughter Marjorie (b 1904) and son John Wallace (b 1907) in the back garden of the house in 1907. As business boomed the family grew wealthier and Wallace commissioned the building of a bigger and much grander house on Tedgness Road in Upper Padley, Grindleford. They named it 'Westwood' (since renamed 'Longacres'). This was the first private house ever to be built with a steel frame.

Wallace's national profile was also growing. He became the first Secretary of the Photographic Dealers' Association when it was formed in 1914, its President in 1920 and Honorary Secretary from 1925-36. He was also a very prominent figure in the Masonic movement. He was Master of his lodge in Sheffield and for many years a member and officer of the Grand Lodge in London.

The Sheffield business continued to thrive and more shops were purchased in Rotherham, Worksop and Retford, but Wallace had bigger ambitions. In 1919, just after the end of the First World War, he opened a

*'Westwood' Tedgness Road in Upper Padley, Grindleford.*

shop on New Bond Street in London and named it Wallace Heaton Ltd. There were six staff and the business would grow to employ 350 by the time of his death in 1957. It was in the 1920s and '30s that Heaton's became a household name for photography. He advertised on the back of horse-drawn cabs and buses, so that the company was always visible. The humour continued; during the Second World War, when rationing was most strict, he apparently ran an advert saying, 'Buy a microscope and see your meat ration!' He expanded the range of goods on sale to include the very best cameras, microscopes and lenses, supplying the Royal Family as well as professional photographers.

The family moved from Derbyshire to Wimbledon and by 1928 Wallace Heaton had bought 'The Black Hut' near Newdigate, an impressive country house with a 138 acre shoot. The following year he acquired City Sale and Exchange Ltd. and diversified his business into the sale of gramophone records, another astute business decision given the growing popularity of recorded music. He was one of the country's first record dealers. Business boomed and by 1934 Wallace had bought another property, 'Wephurst Park' at Wisboro Green, a 600 acre working farm.

*Wallace outside his Bond Street shop*

Wallace Heaton's catalogue and price list, The Blue Book, was published every year from 1949-1972. It was a reference book for keen photographers and showed the very comprehensive range of goods available. The company received its first Royal Warrant from HRH the Prince of Wales in 1932 and held it for over two decades. Wallace Heaton photographed the Royal Family and also supplied them with cameras and equipment, teaching the Queen Mother, the young Queen Elizabeth and Prince Philip how to use them.

He died in 1957 aged 79 and had been working in his office until just a few days before his death. A letter of condolence was sent to his family by the Queen.

His funeral service paid tribute to his many achievements and his charitable donations to a range of good causes:

*'However much of the success of his business was due to his perception and astuteness, it drew its strength from the qualities of his own character – his integrity, his forthright honesty and his strict regard for upright dealing... It was characteristic of him that he always seemed to have time to do a kindly deed and give help where help was needed'.* Funeral Address given by Dr.Joseph Moffat at St George's Church, Hanover Square, London W1.

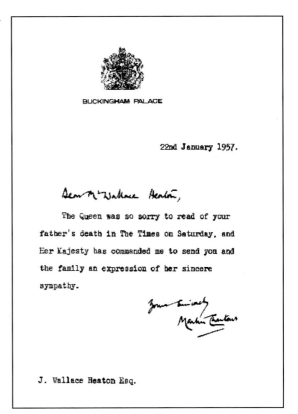

BUCKINGHAM PALACE

22nd January 1957.

Dear Mr Wallace Heaton,

The Queen was so sorry to read of your father's death in The Times on Saturday, and Her Majesty has commanded me to send you and the family an expression of her sincere sympathy.

Yours sincerely
Martin Charteris

J. Wallace Heaton Esq.

*'He stays in the recollection of all who knew him as irrepressively alive - a man fixing his sight on the wide horizon, relentlessly forging ahead and setting the pace for those both marching with him or just following in his footsteps. We feel that the photographic industry as a whole, and in particular his colleagues, have not fully realised as yet how much he achieved, not only for himself but for everyone connected with photography.'* (Amateur Photography obituary)

In 1972 the company was sold to Dixons and, two decades later, photographic processing would change radically with the development of digital photography.

We are very grateful to Wallace Heaton's Grandson, Michael, who kindly supplied the photographs and information for this summary of Wallace's life. Further material can be accessed online at the Heaton family archive.

# OTTAWAY'S NURSERY

## Susan Gudjonsson

This remarkable photograph harks back to a time when allotments, market gardens and nurseries were a feature in Nether Edge. Fresh fruit and vegetables were produced locally, either for personal consumption or for sale in local shops. You have to look very carefully at the photograph below, taken in one of Mr Ottaway's greenhouses in 1906, before you realise what is growing... Yes, cucumbers – and a lot of them!

The lad in the photo is 14 year old Fred Morton, who went on to become a park keeper for Endcliffe, Millhouses and Graves Park. The picture comes courtesy of his grandson, and maybe the man is Mr Ottaway. The firm of J W Ottaway and Son had a nursery for many years on the corner of Oakdale Road and Union Road (where Oakdale and Nether Court flats are now). The nursery was established some time in the 19th century by Alfred Leeming. We know also that Mr Henry Slaney had a market garden at 6 Byron Road (very handy for supplying the local shops!). It's clear too that there was great enthusiasm for both home and allotment gardening, as indicated by the Nether Edge Flower and Horticultural Society, which flourished in Victorian times.

# Part 3

# Education and

# Educationists

*Hunters Bar schoolroom in 1907*

# NETHER EDGE GRAMMAR SCHOOL

## Sarah Matthews with Elizabeth Birks and David Ludham

The building across Union Road from the former Nether Edge Hospital (previously the Ecclesall Union Workhouse) is now converted into flats, but it was built in 1902 to house the Workhouse offices. In between times, as many will remember, it had yet another life as a school.

*Brincliffe Grammar School 1962*

Nether Edge Grammar School (for boys) was established in 1927. As the Union Road building was not ready at the start of the academic year King Edward VII School in Broomhill was the pupils' temporary home until building work was complete. Even when the building was deemed habitable and the pupils were transferred from King Edwards it took time before the school found its feet. Structurally, the school resembled a building site and the noise of workers outside had a habit of seeping through the windows and into the classrooms. The relatively high turnover of headmasters in the early years also suggests that the school was undergoing some trial and error before it established itself as a stable and reputable institution.

Outdoor space on the school site was somewhat limited, and so the gym was fully utilised as a space where students could eat and play on their breaks. Luckily the school sports field, located between Springfield Road and Carterknowle Road, was not too far away for those willing to take the short trip across Brincliffe Fields. Once there, they could make full use of the football and cricket pitches, which were likely to have been used by various other local schools, but were ultimately known as Nether Edge fields. Other opportunities to meet pupils from neighbouring schools came on the weekends in the form of inter-school games of football and cricket. Those attending in the later years also have memories of the annual athletics and cross country events. For athletics, pupils were divided and competed by house. House names at Nether Edge did not follow conventional lines, and were named after historical and regional peoples such as the Egyptians, Romans, Greeks, Irish, Welsh and others. One disadvantage for those without the funds, or for students more generally as war pushed on, was the scarceness of the necessary equipment to compete. Some were lucky enough to have an older brother's plimsolls to borrow for the day, whereas others who were less fortunate had no choice but to sit aside and watch.

School life back across at Union Road followed the same structure and procedure as most other schools. On admission to the school at age eleven, the boys found themselves in one of three forms in their year group, each consisting of around thirty students in total. Whether a student found themselves in form 1A, 1B or 1C was dependent on their performance in their 11+ examination, and they would remain part of their allocated form right through until their fifth year where all pupils were then split between two forms. Another consistent feature of school life, aside from forms, was the 9am assembly in the hall each morning, lead by the headmaster. The assembly would usually consist of hymns, prayers and any addresses or notices that the headmaster sought to make the school aware of. Tragically, during wartime, some of these addresses would be passing on the sad news of Old Boys who had been killed in the war. After assembly, classes would take pupils up until lunch at midday. By that point, there were around three or four periods to go before school finished at 4pm, although these times did vary slightly over the years.

In 1957 Nether Edge Grammar School changed its name and moved to its new building as Abbeydale Grammar School – subsequently merging with the adjacent girls' Grange Grammar to form the late lamented Abbeydale Grange comprehensive.  But the Union Road building didn't remain empty. Between 1957 and 1965 it housed the new and short-lived Brincliffe Grammar School, set up to relieve the burden of the postwar baby boom and to accommodate students of the Junior College of Art who had moved from the city centre. The first intake was all girls aged 13, but from 1958 it took a mixed intake of 11+. On comprehensivisation in 1965 Brincliffe itself closed, and the building became Sheffield Education Department's Media Centre.

---

**Here are Denise West's memories** of transferring from High Storrs to become one of Brincliffe Grammar School's first students.

I grew up in Crookes. I had a happy childhood though books and learning didn't feature much. I was the only one in our primary school to pass the 11+ and some of the other pupils took against me. In 1956 I started at High Storrs Grammar school which was a frightening experience since I knew nobody, but during the two years I was there I made three good girl friends.

1957-58 was the year that the post-war 'bulge' hit secondary schools. Extra places had to be found across the city. In my second year at High Storrs the girls were asked if anyone would like to transfer at 13 to a new all-girls grammar on Union Road, Nether Edge. Nether Edge Grammar, which had occupied the building since the 1920s had moved out in July 1957 to their new premises at Abbeydale. The Union Road school reopened in September of the same year with a new name - Brincliffe Grammar School.

My friends decided to transfer and I wanted to be with them and so, despite the prospect of either an hour-long journey with two buses or a long walk and the circular bus, I enrolled that September in Year 3 (now called year 9). The entrance was right opposite the gates of Nether Edge Hospital. Year 3 was the only intake that year - around 50 girls in all, drawn mainly from the south-west of the city and divided into two classes according to age. I was born in July so I was put in 3B with Mrs Dixon. I never got to know her very well since she never taught me.

I hated the uniform which was a bulky grey pinafore over either a pullover or a tee-shirt in house colours. We had dark green blazers, berets and gabardine macs. In summer we wore green and white check dresses. The punishment was severe if we were spotted en-route to and from school without our berets on.

The following year, 1958, there was a larger, mixed intake at age 11. So we were always three years older than the class below and of course we had no -one older than ourselves to look up to. I can't remember any out of school activities, and there was no mixing with other schools or the local community. I suppose I accepted it at the time but looking back it was a very narrow experience.

It was a strange time - despite the school having only about 50 pupils in 1957 we were allocated a prefabricated classroom by the side of the main school. This was because renovation work was taking place in the main building. It was a traditional school - large teaching rooms with high ceilings opening off a central hall, on two floors. We also used two buildings over the road by the bus stop. But in our first year the staff came to our classroom rather than us doing the moving around. We had desks in which we kept our books. The school opened straight onto Union Road so we just had a yard at the back which we walked around at break-time. There was a gym with all the usual equipment, including hula hoops, but for other sports we needed to get the bus up to High Storrs. School dinners were provided in the hall but in fine weather my friends and I were permitted to take our packed lunches up to Chelsea Park. We had milk at morning break time. With the bus-stop being just outside I never got to explore Nether Edge, but I do recall there was a printing company in the old chapel next door to the school and a sweet shop on the corner.

The school was run on traditional lines. There were four houses named after forests - Arden, Dean, Epping and Sherwood- with captains and vice-captains, and there was a prefect system. The staff comprised seven men and about 13 women. Those who were graduates wore their gowns. The headteacher, Mr Hill, Mr Spinks (Maths) and maybe some others had previously taught boys on the same site, other teachers transferred in and yet others were straight from teacher training. The deputy head was Mrs Potter who taught English. I was good at English so she never bothered me but other girls were regularly reduced to tears. I regretted the absence of drama which I had enjoyed at High Storrs. Miss Bingham taught languages but only Spanish was offered and later Italian. Mr Boole who taught science was okay but I grew to dislike the Maths teacher which largely resulted in my failing the O level. Those who taught me were nearly all disciplinarians who made frequent use of sarcasm. I don't remember any beatings but girls were publicly humiliated, 'lines' were handed out and there were frequent detentions. I generally stayed out of trouble and learned to keep a low profile, with the result that the staff never really got to know me properly. One school report led my father to ask me if I was actually going to Geography lessons because the teacher had written that he didn't know who I was!

After the first year we were streamed and I was careful to stay in the B stream since I did not want to be labelled a 'swot'. We chose our options - I discontinued applied subjects and concentrated for my O levels on English, Maths, three sciences, Geography, History and Spanish. I recall that homework was often affected by a shortage of books.

Despite doing 'hard' subjects the teachers made very little effort to disguise their low expectations of me. I was told that I would never pass my O-levels so the staff must have got quite a shock when I passed in eight subjects, achieving top grades in English Language and Literature. Maybe the staff thought that pupils who got in to grammar school at 13+ were academically inferior, or maybe they chose to treat girls differently from the boys they were used to - I will never know, but the general understanding seemed to be that we would not cope with higher education and therefore there was no point in going on to sixth-form.

Having been thus labelled as 'non-academic' I left school at 16 and went to work, first in a laboratory and then in the personnel department at the Yorkshire Electricity Board. By the time I was 20 I was married and soon after that I was expecting a baby which meant I had to give up my job. It was around then that I realised that I was actually pretty bright and that there should be more to life than domesticity. I wanted to train as a teacher. So I went to study A level English and Geography at Sheffield College where for the first time someone took an interest in me and encouraged me to apply for University. After getting a good degree I travelled to Huddersfield daily to do teacher training, followed by several teaching posts in Sheffield schools and colleges.

Looking back, I feel I made the wrong decision to transfer to Brincliffe. I have no happy memories of that school because it did not help me to develop as an individual. The school closed when the Comprehensive system came in and the building became the Education Department Audio Visual Aids Centre and the home of other advisory staff. But I am still in touch with the three friends who transferred with me.

As told to Shelagh Woolliscroft

# THE GLAUERTS, A German family in Nether Edge – John Baxendale

When it went on the market newly-built in 1861, 21 Kenwood Park Rd (known as Cleveland House) was described as an 'excellent stone-built Gothic villa', commanding 'very extensive and beautiful views over Meersbrook and the Derbyshire moors', and all within a few minutes' walk of the Sharrow omnibus – a snip at £650. For a while it belonged to the cutlery manufacturer William Webster, who went on to build himself a big new house on Priory Road, and the Lantern Theatre. By 1901 No 21 was the home of the Glauerts, one of the most interesting of Kenwood's business families – although in the end their achievements were more in the field of science than business.

*Ludwig Glauert*

Louis Glauert (1846-1919) and his younger brother Carl arrived in Sheffield from Oldenberg in Germany in 1872 to set up a cutlery firm. Moving from one factory to another as their business grew, L and C Glauert ended up at Wallace Works on Furnival St near the city centre. They seem to have been involved in many branches of the cutlery trade, but especially in the production of 'German forks', described as having 'flat shank and bib', over which they claimed copyright. No doubt the German connection remained important: in 1877 Louis returned to Germany and came back married to

*21 Kenwood Park Road*

Amanda Watkinson, who was English but born in Hamburg, where her father Samuel had moved his cutlery business in the 1850s. Both brothers joined the Freemasons and became naturalised British subjects.

Sadly Carl died in 1891 aged only 42, but not before marrying Clara Colver, a farmer's daughter, but also a member of one of Sheffield's most prominent business families –

*Hermann Glauert*

a useful connection for any rising Sheffield businessman.

By this time Louis and Amanda were living in Nether Edge, at 17 Glen Rd, where four of their five children were born in quick succession: Ludwig (1879), Otto (1881), Elsa (1882) and Gertrud (1883) – and then after a long interval, Hermann (1892). Clearly the family needed and could now afford a larger house, and by 1891 they were at 21 Kenwood Park Rd, which remained the family home until Amanda died in 1925.

But it was the children who made the Glauerts unusual. Instead of following the usual pathway of the family firm or local professions, four of them went to university and achieved academic distinction in science and mathematics. Ludwig, like his brothers, attended local preparatory schools in Kenwood and went on to Sheffield Royal Grammar School on Collegiate Crescent (later King Edward VII).

As a teenager he was a keen member of the Sheffield Naturalists' Club, and a noted chess player. After achieving first class honours in Geology at the then Sheffield University College, he worked for a while as a demonstrator in the Metallurgy Department, and then in his father's firm. But Geology and Natural History were closest to his heart, and in 1908 he went to work for the West Australia Mines Department where he could pursue these interests. He made his name as a palaeontologist for his work on Australian fossils and living animals including scorpions and reptiles, and eventually became Director of the Western Australia Museum, where he displayed his passion for engaging the public in the world of science and nature.

Otto won first prize in mathematics and a prestigious scholarship at Clare College, Cambridge in 1900, and played chess for the University. But his academic career was dogged by ill-health, and he emerged with a third class degree and a career as a schoolmaster, though producing significant work in the field of aeronautics, no doubt inspired by his brother Hermann.

Hermann's career was a glittering one, though tragically short. After winning the prestigious Open Mathematics Scholarship at Trinity College, Cambridge he took several important prizes for Mathematics and Astronomy, and was a Wrangler in 1913: Cambridge's way of saying that he got a First in Maths. He became a Fellow of Trinity and intended to become an astronomer, but, perhaps unhappy languishing in Cambridge during the War because of his German ancestry, he switched fields and took a post at the Royal Aircraft Establishment at Farnborough, where he became Principal Scientific Officer and one of the foremost pioneers in the new field of aerodynamics, developing theory that was crucial to future aircraft design, before being killed in a freak accident in 1934, while out for a walk with his family and his brother Otto. He was only 42.

I have left the two girls to last because in many ways their careers were the most interesting. Elsa's time at Sheffield High School was covered in scholarly glory, and she arrived at Girton College, Cambridge in 1900 full of promise. At this time the talk was all of the suffrage and the 'New Woman'. When Elsa completed her course in 1904 she was the great hope of the feminists, and a large crowd of women assembled to hear her results. Cambridge did not give women degrees until 1948, but in a typically English fudge they were told what degree they would have got: Elsa would have been a Wrangler, and was the best female mathematician of her year. However, unlike her brothers, she did not seek to climb further in the academic world but began a successful career as a school teacher, eventually in 1922 becoming Head of the new Scarborough Girls High School, where she remained until she retired in 1946. I have it on good authority that her colleagues, in recognition of the unfairness of Elsa not receiving a Cambridge degree, refused to wear their own academic gowns.

And Gertrud, what of her? It is, alas, an all too familiar story. She never married, or went to university, but remained at home in Kenwood Park Road with her ageing parents and after they died went to live in Cambridge with Hermann's widow Muriel – herself a scientist of some repute, as were her and Hermann's three children, and poor uncle Carl's only son.

At the end of the nineteenth century there was a lot of talk about German competition and in particular Germany's superior focus on technical and scientific education. The Sheffield industries were inherently scientific, and many businessmen's sons took qualifications in chemistry or metallurgy at the newly established Sheffield University, before joining the family firm. That the Glauerts (or most of them) climbed higher, and away from Sheffield, I am sure owes a great deal to their German cultural heritage.

# PROFESSOR WILLIAM RIPPER, ENGINEER

## Kay Phillips and John Austin

Professor William Ripper lived on Meadow Bank Avenue from 1912 to 1936. He was not a native of Sheffield but had moved to the city in 1874. Local directories show that he had lived in Crookesmoor, Western Bank and Wellesley Road before his move to Nether Edge. In 1912 he bought two newly-built, semi-detached, Edwardian villas (numbers 41 and 43) on the north side of Meadow Bank Avenue.

Professor Ripper played a very significant role in developing technical education in Sheffield and in establishing the University of Sheffield's reputation as a respected centre for engineering education and research. In recent years the University has invested heavily in building stronger links with industry, collaborating to support the development of cutting-edge engineering technologies and improving educational pathways for engineering apprentices and graduates. The Advanced Manufacturing Research Centre is a very visible sign of its success. In many ways these developments mirror the work of William Ripper.

His early life was spent in the south west of England. Born in Plymouth in 1853, he was educated there and in Exeter before returning to his home town to become an engineering apprentice. He also worked for a marine engineering company in Stockton-on-Tees. He was nineteen when he won a Queen's Scholarship to attend Exeter Teacher Training College. This would be turning point for William; two years later in 1874 he arrived in Sheffield as an Assistant Master, employed by the Sheffield School Board. Sir John Brown was Chairman of the Board and he arranged to have classes for engineering artisans at Carbrook School. William Ripper taught them Machine Construction, Drawing and The Steam Engine. He must have made a strong impression because within a year, at the age of twenty two, he was Headmaster of the Walkley Board School, a position he occupied for the next five years on an annual salary of £110.

*Firth College, Leopold Street.*

Significantly he also taught classes at the Mechanics' Institute.

The opening of the Central Higher Grade Board School was very significant for science education in Sheffield. In 1880 William Ripper became the Central School's Science Master and he continued to organise evening classes at the old Firth College. Very bright pupils were attracted to the courses and the pioneering opportunities to work in Science Laboratories and Manual Training Workshops. This change in education was prompted by a fear that other countries were moving ahead of Britain with better designs and lower prices for their products. Ripper's commitment to the Technical Movement was crucial. The numbers of students accessing the courses increased year on year and new staff were recruited to meet the demand. Local benefactors like Sir F.T.Mappin provided the funding to buy whatever equipment was required.

In 1884 a Department of Metallurgy and Engineering was added to the College. W.H. Greenwood became the Professor of Metallurgy and Principal of the College: William Ripper was chosen as his deputy, becoming Professor of Engineering. This new department grew into the Sheffield Technical School and in 1889 William Ripper was its Principal. A year later he was offered the chance to develop a complete system of technical education by the Government of New Zealand. Initially he accepted what must have been a tempting opportunity – but when his Sheffield salary was doubled to persuade him to stay here he withdrew his acceptance.

During the late 1880s he began to write textbooks to support technical education. These were published by Longmans, Green and Co. as part of their Elementary Science Manuals series. Technology was changing fast and Ripper's books were repeatedly updated and reprinted. Between 1889 and 1907 his 'Elementary Steam' volume was reprinted 11 times, with three new editions containing additional chapters. In 1909 the title was changed to 'Heat Engines' because of the need for more focus on new engines, notably the internal combustion engine.

As well as leading the Technical Education movement Ripper championed the campaign for pollution control and cleaner air. He believed that science and industry had to work together and lectured on 'Smoke Prevention in Sheffield' as early as 1892. The city was notoriously dirty; an article in the London Daily Telegraph at that time said 'the nether world had no terrors for Sheffield folk, so hardened were they to perpetual smoke and flame'. His scientific work began to focus on superheated steam and the development of a new twin-cylinder superheated motor as a means of reducing pollution.

Professor Ripper was a founder member of the Sheffield Society of Engineers and amalgamated this body with the Sheffield Metallurgical Society in 1894, becoming its President from 1901-3.

There was an even more significant development in 1897, when the Technical School, Firth College and the Sheffield School of Medicine were united and consolidated as the Sheffield University College. The funding for the University College came in part from public donations and William Ripper was praised by Sir William Clegg for his efforts in convincing the city's manufacturers that they should support the development. Many employers had been hostile to the idea of providing education for their workers but it was the workers themselves who showed their support, by organising penny collections in the factories to fund technical education for all who could benefit from it. The Sheffield Weekly News of December 2nd 1900 wrote, *'Professor Ripper is a moral as well as an intellectual force at the Technical School. He holds that man can be elevated by education, apart from any pecuniary or social uplifting. He would like to see education in England continued beyond the age of 14 or 15, believing that elementary education only supplies the tools for the future student to work with. Ripper had contrasted the situation in England with the Continent, 'where they do not allow a man to consider himself educated unless he has been to a school or training institution until about twenty years of age. Professor Ripper is a member of the Institution of Civil Engineers and Institute of Mechanical Engineers. He is a luminous as well as a voluminous writer. The steam engine is his hobby. He lays his hand upon the engine's pulse and plays familiarly with its pressure gauge'*

In an article in the weekly pamphlet, 'Young Sheffield', Professor Ripper's message to young Sheffielders was clear; *'all the city's central schools, technical schools and colleges etc. are of very little real value, unless a student understands that his progress depends upon himself primarily, and upon his work, and that he must only look upon these institutions as valuable helps, not as substitutes for that personal effort, without which nothing worth having can be acquired'.*

Conditions in the new Electrical Engineering Section of the University were far from grand. In 1902 they had 225 students but only two small rooms, one of which was a cellar. Professor Ripper was a member of the Sheffield Education Committee, Chaired by Sir Henry Stephenson. In October 1903 he represented Sheffield on the Alfred Moseley Commission's visit to America to study technical education in the eastern states.

The University College became the University of Sheffield in 1905 and William Ripper added Dean of the Faculty of Applied Science to his Professorial role. An Honorary Doctorate in Engineering was awarded to him in 1908. A second Honorary Doctorate was awarded by the University of Bristol in 1912.

When the First World War broke out Professor Ripper played his part by serving as Vice-Chairman of the Sheffield Munitions Committee, which met every day at the University. He and his department trained munitions workers and manufactured gauges for military applications. He was made a Companion of Honour in 1917 for his work and when King George V and Admiral Jellicoe visited Sheffield, he showed them round his department.

At that time the Vice Chancellor of the University was H.A.L. Fisher, but he resigned to become Minister of Education in Lloyd George's Government. Professor Ripper replaced him, serving as VC for two years before returning to his passion of engineering in 1919. During this time he also served on the City's Commission for Peace.

William Ripper's efforts to bridge the gap between science and industry led to the creation of the Trades Technical Societies. The role of these societies was to help workers who were neither members of scientific societies nor students. They began as a series of public meetings and discussions for workmen in the cutlery, file and tool industries. From these developed regular courses and formal societies for men unused to study, but of considerable skill and experience. By 1950 there were 25 of these societies in

Sheffield alone and many more across the country.

From 1919 Ripper was Professor of Mechanical Engineering and Dean of the Faculty of Engineering. He continued to publish books on engineering, machine drawing and design, and practical chemistry. Retiring in 1923 at the age of 70, he remained an Emeritus Professor of Engineering and Advisor in Technology and lived on Meadow Bank Avenue until 1936. He died aged 84 in Brighton, at his daughter's home, on 13th August 1937. He was buried at Fulwood Church.

**Sources:** William Ripper,  'Heat Engines (Being a new edition of Steam)' Longmans' Elementary Science Manuals, 1909.

*'Young Sheffield'* Pamphlet, 1900

Sheffield Weekly News, December 22nd 1900

University of Sheffield Magazine, Volume 1, Number 1, 1937 - Obituary

University of Sheffield Newsletter, April 1980.

---

# JOAN FLETT, LOCAL HISTORIAN

# Chris Venables

*"Joan was one of the leading lights in the previous Nether Edge History Group, the author of publications on Cherry Tree Hill and the Workhouse, and a key contributor to They Lived in Nether Edge and Sharrow (1988).  We owe a great deal to her work and her inspiration"* John Baxendale.

Joan Flett was born in London in 1923 and she started working at the GEC Laboratories in Wembley at the beginning of the Second World War.  She loved her work, being deployed first on light bulb

*Joan Flett, 2010*

testing and then supporting ground-breaking X-ray crystallography research, despite her young age helping some of those foremost in the field.  She was lucky to meet the Joliot-Curies (Marie Curie's daughter and son-in-law) when they were being shown round the GEC.

She married Tom in 1948, having first met him at primary school and then later through their mutual interest in Scottish dancing.   Whilst Tom completed his PhD in mathematics, they lived in Cambridge and Joan worked in Trinity College library to make ends meet. They moved to Wallasey when Tom began lecturing at Liverpool University. With her background in developing X-ray films, Joan went to work for Kodak and the eminent photographers, Burrell and Hardman. In the 2010s, Joan returned to the Hardman's house on Rodney Street, Liverpool now preserved by the National Trust, and was pleased that it was just as she remembered it in the 1950s.

In 1967, following Tom's appointment as Professor of Pure Mathematics at Sheffield University, they moved to Sheffield and lived initially in a flat on Sharrow Lane while they house hunted. Settling on Nether Edge as the best place to live, it took a year to find their Kingfield Rd house with large garden which Joan tended with such pride even in her late 80s, long after Tom had died early in 1976.

So where did Joan's particular interest in local history come from? Joan used to go English folk dancing and she and Tom were experts on the history of traditional dancing, having started their own pioneering field research with a trip to the Hebrides in 1953. They published their first book in 1964, the definitive 'Traditional Dancing in Scotland' and Joan went on to publish a further two books on dancing after Tom's death.

Turning to researching local history was a natural move for Joan with more time on her hands as her daughters left home. After Tom's death, Joan started working at Nether Edge Hospital, and, having become interested in its history, she wrote, 'The Story of the Workhouse and Hospital at Nether Edge', to raise funds for the Friends of the Hospital. Following the formation of the Nether Edge Neighbourhood Group Local History Section in 1982, Joan produced her first book with the Local History Section entitled 'They lived in Sharrow and Nether Edge', which according to Amazon has sold some 6,000 copies since it was first published in 1988. The book was used as a precedent for this current book about people and places.

Her last book on Nether Edge was 'Cherry Tree Hill and the Newbould Legacy' published in 1999. This was the result of fortuitously living in the last house to be sold from the Elizabeth Newbould Estate and thereby receiving with the house deeds all of the documents relating to the sale of the entire estate dating back to 1702. She continued to be interested in local activities and in 2008, to celebrate the 35th anniversary of NENG, she wrote the preface to the Nether Edge History Group's 'Old Sharrow and Nether Edge in Photographs' (2nd edition). Pleased to record that George

Wolstenholm's home and the Kenwood area with its tree lined streets had changed little, she wrote of new housing anticipated as Sheffield Hallam University were vacating the old Bluecoat School site.

Joan became involved with the Nether Edge Neighbourhood Group when it was formed in 1973, helping wherever she could as well as keeping a weather eye on planning issues and campaigning to preserve the older properties in Nether Edge. She worked hard to ensure that the former Victorian Workhouse/ Nether Edge Hospital site (bought by Gleeson Homes in 1997) wasn't turned into a giant housing estate and was delighted when Nether Edge became a Conservation Area in September 2002. She was appointed NENG's Chairman in 1976, Vice Chairman in 1979, Secretary 1981 -1987 and Chairman again 2001- 4.

*Traditional Heritage Museum, Ecclesall Rd, 2008*

Joan was also active at the Traditional Heritage Museum – Sheffield's "Secret Museum" on Ecclesall Rd., which was established by Prof. John Widdowson and opened to the public in 1985. During the Sunday openings she could normally be found welcoming visitors and showing them the "shops" which had been re-created by Harry Pearson, Malcolm Weston and others. She particularly liked the "basket makers, clog-makers, pawnbrokers, high-class grocers and posh parlour with a small harmonium used in Ecclesall Parish Church until the 1970's."

She was very disappointed when, due to structural problems, the museum closed in 2011 and some 46,000 items were put into storage pending their transfer to other sites. Many of the museum's domestic household items, covering the period 1850 – 1970, went to Green Estate, who run Sheffield Manor Lodge, to form part of the site's WW2 Living History Cottages (on Manor Lane, S2).

Until 2013, still keen to make use of her research skills, Angus Hunter remembers, "sharing the General Cemetery Gatehouse office with her on many a cold morning" as she spent two mornings a week transcribing microfiche records of burials for family history research for the Sheffield General Cemetery Trust and visitors. She produced a number of articles for their magazine *'Undertakings'* on notable cemetery 'residents' and went on to write, together with Jean Lees and Tanya Schmoller, 'Post Mortem', a book on interesting people buried in the Cemetery associated with the Medical profession.

Joan ran the Nether Edge Neighbourhood Group's Luncheon Club for the housebound at Shirley House for 30 years – co-ordinating the food, entertainment and attendees. Sue Bolger remembers,

*"I became a volunteer driver after moving to Sheffield, brought my youngest on the trips, and made a lot of friends. The luncheon club folded when the cooks became older and more tired than the dwindling attendees: some were well over 80 yrs. Joan was much admired and sometimes frightened of as she ran a tight ship!"*

We would like to acknowledge the help from Joan's daughters Jane Harrison and Lindsay Smith in researching this article.

*Joan's family planting a copper beech tree in Chelsea Park in memory of her.*

---

# TANYA SCHMOLLER

## Kay Phillips

Tanya Schmoller lived in Nether Edge from 1985 until her death, at the age of 97, in January 2016. She was an active member of the community and a familiar face at local events, but relatively few people would have been aware of what she had achieved during her long life. For a woman of her era Tanya's story is remarkable; in the words of a family member, she was, 'highly independent, determined and intrepid'. These traits were visible from a young age and were evident throughout her life.

Born in Uruguay in South America, she was the daughter of an English mother – Violet Pitt, and Russian father – Tomas Randers Kent. Tanya's mother had left England for Argentina to be with her sister and to help look after her children. The sister was married to an English engineer who had gone to Buenos Aires to work on the development of Argentina's railways. The stone for the railway came from a quarry in Uruguay, in the village of Conchillas, across the River Plate from Buenos Aires. This was where the man who would become Tanya's father was employed as a book-keeper, managing orders for the stone. He became a friend of the British engineer and his family, including Tanya's mother.

*Tanya pictured at her home in Rundle Road, 2015*

*(photographer Jeremy Abrahams)*

Tomas was an educated man who had studied in Heidelberg. What brought him to Uruguay is unknown, but Russia was a dangerous place in the last years of the Tsarist regime, particularly for those seeking political change. Interviewed by photographer Jeremy Abrahams shortly before she died Tanya said. 'He told me that he had to leave Russia for good, but I didn't have the sense to ask him why.'

Violet and Tomas married and had four children. Tanya was born in Conchillas on the 3rd March 1918 and named Tatyana Mary Kent; three brothers followed. The family was poor, living in a small single-storey house with earth floors. The children attended the local village primary school but Tanya's secondary education was at the British School in Montevideo, paid for by her father's employer. She was a tall, confident and bright student who was also good at sports, a keen swimmer and winner of athletics trophies. During this time, Tanya attended the first World Cup Final in Montevideo (1930) and she would be a lifelong supporter of Uruguay's national team.

Leaving school in 1935 aged 17, Tanya worked in an office in Buenos Aires to support her family. Her father had died when she was 16 but

*Tanya as a schoolgirl c1934*

her mother decided to stay in Uruguay. When the Second Word War broke out, she returned to Uruguay and took a job with Uruguayan Railways, where the Manager was working for MI5 as its representative in Uruguay. Tanya assisted him but resigned from her job over a major disagreement with her boss; she had taken a stand against antisemitism following the expulsion of two Jewish children from the British School.

By 1944 she was working for the British Council in Montevideo and it was here that she was asked to be a guide for Allen Lane, founder of Penguin Books, who was visiting Uruguay to assess the market for Penguin's titles. It was a meeting that would change her life. Tanya was an avid reader of Penguin Books and she impressed Lane with her knowledge. She told

*Tanya during her time at Penguin*

him that her ambition was to study at the London School of Economics and he clearly saw her potential. Lane offered her the chance to work for him in London and agreed to fund night school classes at the LSE. Tanya immediately accepted and soon began to plan her move to England.

The journey wasn't straightforward but it demonstrated Tanya's independent, determined spirit. It would take her three months via a series of flights through Chile, Peru, Venezuela, Mexico, Cuba, and Miami, to New York. Then, in the absence of Atlantic air crossings, she boarded a troop ship to Southampton and, at the end of 1945, began working for Lane as his personal assistant.

Nicholas Barker's obituary for Tanya in The Independent described her contribution to Penguin:

'*The Penguin offices were in Harmondsworth, where she started on £6 a week. She lived nearby with the Lane family at Silverbeck. She was as ready to work on Lane's farm as to write letters for him, working 8-6 at the office and often on into the evening. Lane came to value her judgement on books, people and any project that came his way. She never asserted herself, but her opinions were firm and crisply expressed. She became a reader* (especially of Spanish books), and an editor in her own right. She met the authors of Pelican books, among them Karl Popper, her teacher at the LSE. She also did evening classes at the London School of Printing.'

In 1949, Hans Schmoller came to Penguin to succeed the legendary Jan Tschichold as chief designer, and Tanya and he were married the next year. Hans was an exile from Germany, a survivor of the Nazi Holocaust, which had taken the lives of both of his parents.  He had been working in Basutoland, running the French Protestant Mission Press. An eminent typographer, he would go on to become Art Director of Penguin Books. Tanya had already become second mother to Hans' young daughter Monica, (his first wife had died in 1948), who was now joined by a son, Sebastian. In between bringing them up, Tanya kept her connection with Penguin, in 1958 resuming work to take charge of Lane's correspondence. This was a formidable task during the furore over the Lady Chatterley's Lover trial in 1960, from which Penguin emerged victorious. She continued to work closely with Lane until his death in 1970.'

The Schmollers collaborated on a number of important projects. One notable example was the development of The Complete Pelican Shakespeare (1969-72); Hans was its designer and Tanya undertook all the proofreading. She retired from Penguin in 1975.

In the family home on the Thames the couple had shelves full of Penguin books. They decided to try to put together a complete set of every book that bore the Penguin name and logo, and in 1979 they gave the almost complete collection of 11,000 books to the London School of Economics. The Schmollers also worked together to amass an important collection of decorated papers used mainly for book covers, and endpapers. Through this work Tanya developed a network of contacts with notable artists, for example Tirzah Garwood, wife of Eric Ravilious.

In 1985, the Fifty Penguin Years exhibition opened at the Royal Festival Hall, marking the significance of the publications which had made books affordable to a wider public. Sadly this was also the year in which Hans died. Two and a half years later Tanya

*Tanya with Monica and Sebastian*

moved to Sheffield to be closer to her son Seb, Sarah Blandy and their two children.

Her passion for learning continued undimmed in later life. Tanya studied for both a BSc Honours degree and a BA Honours with the Open University, receiving her awards in 1999 and 2003 at the ages of 81 and 85 respectively. She also continued to write articles on the subject of decorated paper. The Schmoller Collection of decorated papers was given to Manchester Metropolitan University and, in recognition of her work in curating it Tanya received an Honorary Doctorate from the University on her 90th birthday.

*Honorary Doctorate award, 2008*

In 2008 she also published a memoir entitled Penguin Days for the Penguin Collectors Society, of which she was a founder member. The book contains extracts from over 200 weekly letters written to her mother in Uruguay. It is a fascinating read and illustrates the wide range of her work for Penguin and the various circles into which she connected; academic, literary, artistic, political and diplomatic.

Politically Tanya was firmly on the left and was a committed member of the Labour Party; in 1999 she received an Award of Merit from the then Minister for the Regions, Richard Caborn MP. She was also a long-serving supporter of CND and during the 1980s went with Sarah to take part in the women's protest at Greenham Common. Although she wouldn't necessarily describe herself as a feminist Tanya was a strong, independent woman with a determination to achieve the goals she set for herself.

She was active in the Nether Edge Neighbourhood Group for many years, as a distributor of EDGE and supporter of NENG's activities. Perhaps her greatest contribution to local history was the archival work that she did for The General Cemetery Trust. Over a period of twenty years Tanya helped to transcribe 87,000 burial records. Working with a small team of volunteers, every single record was put onto a database. New knowledge on topics such as the 'African village' in Attercliffe and common causes of female deaths emerged from this important research. In recognition of her commitment Tanya was given a civic award by the Lord Mayor just after her 90th birthday.

Tanya Schmoller was someone who had friends all over the world. On the face of it she might appear to be quiet and private, but she had a genuine interest in people and often maintained strong links with those she met. One example was a Japanese family with whom she became firm friends. This stemmed from a chance conversation at the bus stop with a man who was a visiting scholar at the University of Sheffield. It led to reciprocal visits to each other's homes.

Above all she took great delight in her family. Gatherings with her children, grandchildren and greatgrandchildren form the subject of many of the photographs which the family discovered after her death. She is pictured dressing up, playing board games, doing cryptic crosswords, enjoying days on the beach, in the garden and walks in the country. In almost every picture she still has the smile and direct gaze of the talented young woman who won so many prizes at her school in Montevideo.

With grateful thanks to the Schmoller family, Seb, Monica, Sarah, and Jacob for their help in providing additional information and photographs for this profile of Tanya.

---

# BARBARA FORD

## Kath Fry

This is Barbara Ford's story as told to me in 2016. Part of it appears in *'Aspects of Nether Edge'*, published in 2017, in the chapter 'The Ecclesall Bierlow 'Nether Edge' Workhouse, 'Heaven' or 'Hell'?

In 1931, Barbara was born to her unmarried mother in a mother and baby home in Leeds. This was just a few years after the care of the poor had been transferred from the Guardians of the Poor to Sheffield Corporation, which could be said to mark the end of the ramifications of The New Poor Law, in theory if not in actuality. In Victorian times Barbara would have been described as a workhouse baby, a pauper, for at the age of three and a half her mother handed her over to the care of Sheffield Public Assistance Board who placed her in a Fulwood Cottage Home, at Lodge Moor. Prior to 1903 a child in Barbara's situation would have been housed in the Ecclesall Bierlow Union workhouse on Union Road, Nether Edge, Sheffield, for it is the Ecclesall Bierlow Guardians who had built the Cottage homes to take the workhouse children out to the outskirts of the city and fresh air.

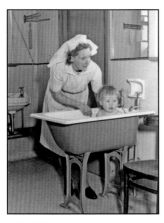

*Bathtime at the Fulwood Cottage Home.*

Barbara is not her original name; it was given her by the nuns at her birth place, for reasons unknown to her. Barbara was later told that on her arrival at the Cottage Home she cried for three days, and could not be comforted. That was the last Barbara saw of her mother, save for one visit when she was eleven years old. This was when she met Rosemary, the sister aged six she never knew she had, also illegitimate, who had come to join her at Lodge Moor. Rosemary was greatly distressed to be at the Cottage Home, and her new found sister became distressed herself as a result. 'My mother had been a naughty girl", says Barbara.

Though purpose built, Barbara says the Cottage Home was cold on winter nights with frost on the bedroom windows in the mornings. Sanitation was basic, with an outdoor privy and a communal chamber pot in the bedroom for night-time use. Barbara shared a bedroom with six other children, seven others slept in another bedroom with a third for the foster mother. She remembers twenty 'cottages' like this on the site. Those numbered one to nine housed the boys and ten to nineteen the girls. Number twenty was home to the babies, aged up to three years of age.

The children wore a uniform at all times, a dark tunic type dress, white blouse and a coloured apron. On Sundays they wore a less formal dress with a white apron. No cardigans were worn. All the girls were dressed identically, even down to their hairstyles. Underclothing consisted of vest 'combinations', a Liberty bodice (a tight garment that did up with little rubber buttons), dark knickers with elastic tops and bottoms and black woollen stockings. These rubbed and chafed Barbara and it was not until many years later she discovered she was allergic to wool. A change of underwear was limited to once a week, even though some children wet their knickers and their beds. Barbara leaves the resultant smell to one's imagination. As a result of the cold most children had chilblains, a very painful condition of the fingers and toes that was treated with the application of 'wintergreen' ointment before they went to bed. A bath was weekly, no more, and the bath water was not changed. Barbara remembers what the water was like to be the last one in!

All the children in the house were responsible for the housework and assisting the foster mother with household tasks. The dining/sitting room had a coal fire, and the kitchen a Yorkshire range. It was Barbara's job to clean and 'black lead' the range weekly and polish the large fender that surrounded it. Being given such a regular and menial task may have been the result of Barbara having poor vision for, although being a bright girl, she says that due to her eye problems 'I went from first in the class to the bottom'. She went to a number of schools, not knowing the reason why. First was Mayfield Junior, then Broomhill, followed by Western Road and then Nether Green with her education ending at St Thomas' Church school at the age of fourteen. Barbara recalls this being the best of all the schools she attended.

*Barbara Ford in 2017*

Over the years Barbara had wanted her mother to contact her even though her mother had to all intents and purposes abandoned her girls. Barbara gives no hint of blame or sadness towards her mother except when she talks of the chance she had to be adopted by the loving French couple she knew as a baby. Her voice hardens when she says, *'My mother refused permission'.*

Despite such a disrupted start in life, Barbara has fond memories of growing up, after all, she says, 'It's all I knew.' In Barbara's opinion, the Superintendent and his wife, the Matron, (Mr and Mrs Hildreth) 'deserved a medal'. They knew all the children on the site and treated them all as if they were their own. Food was simple but adequate. The foster mothers were kind although sanctions, which included not being allowed cake and being sent to bed early, were imposed for misbehaviour. Barbara remembers food she could not stand being put back in the larder and repeatedly being served up until she ate it. However there were also treats, outings, parties and Christmas shows. The staff encouraged the Girl Guide movement to play a large part in Barbara's life which has continued to this day and she is still a 'Trefoil' Guide member.

Barbara's sight problem was picked up by the School Health Service and she was put in the care of the optical department of the Royal Infirmary. Instead of being sent to the School for the Blind on Manchester Road the eye specialist decided to monitor Barbara himself, which he did until she was twenty one. On leaving school, Barbara worked as a maid in the Matron's own home, before being sent at eighteen to Thornsett Lodge children's home in High Bradfield. She recalls this as being very hard work. Little three year olds would creep out of bed at night and turn on all the taps! General nurse training at Rotherham followed, leading to midwifery training at the Jessop Hospital and Nether Edge Hospital, which itself had been the original Ecclesall Bierlow workhouse. Barbara was Night Nursing Officer at the Jessop where she was responsible for all the facilities and overnight staff before retiring early at fifty five years of age. However, Barbara's working life had not ended. Being a committed Christian since childhood, she became a missionary with the Baptist Missionary Society and went first to India, to the Berhampur Hospital for Women and Children in Norissa. After this Barbara went to work in Palestine, at the Nazareth Hospital, a charitable institution founded by the Edinburgh Missionary Society in 1881. Barbara was a tutor in both, training local girls to be nurses and midwives.

Barbara now lives an independent life in Nether Edge, with her own apartment in sheltered housing, where she enjoys a happy fulfilled lifestyle. Quite an achievement for a 'child of the parish'.

With grateful thanks to Barbara, for our most enjoyable conversations over tea, and her permission to use her story.

# Part 4
# Wartime

*VE Day Party, Edge Bank, 1945*

# DISASTER ON THE FIRST DAY OF THE SOMME, 1ST JULY 1916

## John Cornwell and Mark Goodwill

The death toll of 20,000 British soldiers on the first day of Douglas Haig's "Great Push" on the Somme was a disaster that touched every community in Britain and Ireland, as well as many towns in the Dominions. Nether Edge was no exception and this is the story of thirteen men from the Nether Edge area who lost their lives on that day in 1916, men who were serving in just one Battalion, one that bore the name Sheffield on its brass epaulet badges. There were other Nether Edge men who were killed in action in the battle or died later of their wounds, whilst serving in other units of the British Army. This, however, is the story of those who volunteered, trained and subsequently fought and were killed serving with the 12th Battalion of the York and Lancaster Regiment, who despite their name were the local regiment for Barnsley, Rotherham and Sheffield.

*York and Lancaster Regiment cap*

This battalion was initially called the "Sheffield University and City Special Battalion" later shortened to Sheffield City Battalion, and was one of the "Pals" battalions that sprang up in late August and early September 1914 driven by the unquestioning patriotic hubris of many young men who wanted to "fight for their country". These Pals' battalions were initially outside the Army's formal structure and were often raised by the City or Town Council and for several months were paid for by the ratepayers of the municipality, but the Sheffield one was even more special. The City Battalion blatantly attempted to recruit Sheffield University students and middle class professionals so that they could do their soldiering along "with members of their own class". Their membership was widened to include clerks, a catch-all phrase for young men who saw themselves as the new middle class, wore a suit, collar and tie to work, and who might be articled to one of the professions, or just doing menial office work.

The western and southern suburbs of Sheffield were ripe recruiting areas for the City Battalion and many young men from Nether Edge were disposed to join this seemingly fashionable battalion of the Regiment, rather than one of the more orthodox Regular, Territorial or Service battalions that were also recruiting in Sheffield in 1914. Leading

*Sheffield City Battalion shoulder title.*

Liberal and Conservative councillors, many the social leaders of the City as well as the political heavyweights, along with the active enthusiasm of the Duke of Norfolk, added their encouragement to the battalion's recruiting drive, whilst the local press and the general public treated the volunteers, who trained at Redmires camp and often marched into the city, as heroes already.

During those days of the autumn, winter and early spring of 1914-1915 the volunteers, who were mostly aged between nineteen and twenty-two, were the talk and toast of Sheffield. Their nemesis came twenty–two months later on a gentle slope leading up to an undistinguished French village called Serre that a German regiment from Baden had turned into an impregnable fortress.

Suffice to say their attack on the 1st of July 1916 was a complete disaster and total failure. The German wire had not been cut except for small corner of their sector, the German infantrymen had not been obliterated by the massive British artillery barrage, and the Sheffield lads were facing murderous fire from a short distance away by six well sited machine guns and German riflemen. Hiding in a shell hole was virtually the only option and the hope that you could crawl back through all the dead bodies when it got dark.

Among the 248 dead, out of an attacking force of just over seven hundred men, was Pte. Frederick Haydn HOBSON of 82 Machon Bank Road who was a bank clerk with the London and Midland Bank. His father William was the manager of a spade and shovel works. Frederick was buried at Railway Hollow Cemetery just behind the British line. Families were given the opportunity to add some words of their own at the bottom of the regulation headstone (they were charged three and a half pence per letter) when the Imperial War Graves Commission (now the Commonwealth WGC) eventually built the beautiful formal cemeteries that are scattered along the line of the battlefields in northern France and Belgium to this day. Frederick's family added the words *"For God and Country"*.  He is also named on the St Andrew's Church memorial plaques that are now in Shirley House on Psalter Lane.

Another member of St. Andrews congregation who was killed at Serre was Pte. Cecil Stanley MASON who lived with his parents, Ben and Edith Mason, at 1 Briar Road prior to joining up. His father Ben was a member of the printing staff on the Sheffield Independent newspaper. Stanley (or Rip as he was known to his comrades) worked as a dental mechanic and was only 20 years old when he was killed on the 1st July 1916. He was killed climbing out of the front line trench by a shell burst and did not even make it into No Man's Land. His body was never recovered and he is commemorated on Edwin Lutyens colossally impressive Memorial to the "Missing of the Somme" at Thiepval, a memorial built on the site of one of the German army's most formidable bastions.

Among those also named on the Thiepval Memorial is Corporal Frederick MATHER who lived at 17 Rampton Road. Among the first to respond to Kitchener's call for volunteers he left his job at the Sheffield Savings Bank in Norfolk Street and joined the Sheffield City Battalion, the 12th Bn Y&L Regiment. Seen as a soldier of considerable ability he had been promoted to corporal by June 1916, some achievement in a battalion of so many educated men, and had been recommended for a commission, as so many of volunteers of the 12th Battalion were between 1914 and 1918.

*Arthur Greensmith (second left) and comrades*

Pte. Norman BEDFORD is also named on the Thiepval Memorial. He lived at 8 Kenwood Road, and was the son of Arthur, an estate agent, and Emily Bedford. He had studied mining engineering at Sheffield University and was working as a mining engineer in 1914 when he was among the first group of men to volunteer for the City Battalion, enlisting at the Corn Exchange on 10 September 1914. He was 25 years old when he was killed and has no known grave.

Among the dead Sheffield soldiers was Pte. Arthur Eric Griffith MOUNTAIN who was only eighteen when he enlisted in November 1915 and had turned nineteen only four days before his death on the 1st of July. Educated at the Ashley House School in Worksop, he was the son of Walter and Mary Mountain of 10 Chelsea Road and had been employed at Geo. Senior and Sons at Ponds Forge, a famous Sheffield steel works, that operated on the site now occupied by the Ponds Forge Swimming complex. The family agony was further compounded when his twin brother Henry MOUNTAIN, who enlisted in the 12th Bn on the same day as Arthur, was killed at Gavrelle, near Arras, on 4th May 1917. The two brothers had only joined the Battalion in France in early June 1916 and although Henry survived the first day of the Somme he was killed ten months later.

Pte. Arthur Clarence GREENSMITH was another mining engineering student at the University of Sheffield who volunteered and enlisted on 11th September 1914, one of the many volunteers connected with the University. He lived at 4 Kenwood Park Road and he served in No.14 Platoon in D Company. He was 22 years old when he was killed at Serre and his body was never found. He too is commemorated on the Thiepval Memorial.

There were two other pairs of brothers from Nether Edge who were both killed on the 1st July while serving with the City Battalion. 2nd Lieut. Charles H. WARDILL was one of six brothers who served in the British Army in the

First World War. They were the children of Sydney and Ethel Wardill of 18 Violet Bank Road in the centre of Nether Edge. Charles was only recently commissioned in 1916 and sent to join the City Battalion and was quite elderly for a subaltern. He had been born in 1877 and was 39 years old at the time of his death on the morning of the 1st July. He too has no known grave and he is also commemorated on the Thiepval memorial.

His brother, Pte. Sidney George WARDILL, was killed on the same day in the abortive attack at Serre. He was married with one child and had moved out of his parents' home and was living with his wife, Ethel, at 136 Club Garden Road in Sharrow. He had been a member of the congregation at Cemetery Road Baptist Church before the war and was a lay preacher and an officer in their Boys' Brigade contingent. He worked for Robert Proctor & Son, drapers, in Fargate and had been an early volunteer in the City Battalion. He also has no known grave and his name is recorded on the Thiepval Memorial underneath the name of his brother.

The two Gunstone brothers of 11 Ashland Rd. were members of a famous Sheffield bakery firm and had both been pupils at King Edward VII School in Broomhill. L/Cpl. Frank Reed GUNSTONE had played in goal for the School Football XI, whilst his brother Pte. William Walter GUNSTONE had represented the school at water polo. They were in the same platoon and as they rose to get out of their trench they were killed by German fire. They are buried where they fell in Luke Copse Cemetery that is situated on the site of the British front line on 1st July 1916. They are buried very close to each other, but surprisingly not side by side, and their parents added to their gravestone the somewhat enigmatic words *"Alleluia, the Lord God omnipotent reigneth".*

Thirteen former pupils of King Edward VII School were killed that day serving in the City Battalion and several others perished in other units elsewhere on the Somme Battlefield. Among the thirteen was Pte. John Leonard THORPE who was killed at the German wire in the first few minutes of the attack. Like many of the dead that morning his body lay out in No Man's Land all through the winter of 1916 -17 because it was too dangerous to try and recover it. When the Germans withdrew back to the newly constructed "Hindenburg" Line in February 1917 -- a strategic move designed to shorten their front

*John Leonard Thorpe.*

because of their heavy casualties at Verdun and on the Somme -- then the bodies could be recovered at last. By then they were little more than skeletons held together by their tattered uniforms and their webbing equipment. John Thorpe was most likely identified from his "dog tags" and he is buried in Queen's Cemetery, Pusieux, along with many other recovered bodies. This cemetery is on the site of No Man's Land at Serre halfway to the German wire, and many Sheffielders are buried there.

Before he volunteered John was articled to the accountancy firm of Franklin, Greening and Co. and lived at the family home, 97 Montgomery Road. He had been a keen sportsman at King Edward's gaining his Colours for Football and Cricket and had left the school in the summer of 1912. He was aged 20 when he was killed.

The Central School also lost several former pupils on the First of July, and according to their War Memorial (that was moved to their new buildings at High Storrs in 1933) 45 of their 161 wartime dead served in the York and Lancaster Regiment. Among the Old Centralians who were killed that day was Henry William WHARTON who had been a pupil at the Leopold Street site, but might well have played football up at High Storrs where the school's new playing fields had been constructed in 1906. He was the son of William and Charlotte Wharton of 84 Sandford Grove Road. His parents had the following words added to his headstone;

*"You Watched For Me But Now I Will Watch For You."*

Henry Wharton was also buried in Queen's Cemetery, Pusieux, as was Lance Corporal Noel WILCOCK a saw handle maker working in his father's workshop. He lived at 5 Priory Road and he was 23 when he was killed. Unfortunately his service records were lost in a Second World War air raid and we have no further information on him.

In July 1916 there were many homes in Nether Edge mourning dead soldiers who had been killed fighting in the Battle of the Somme in many different units, but the losses in the City Battalion are especially poignant. Many of the dead were classified as missing and certainty about their death often came seven or eight months later, dashing the faint hopes of families who were praying for a miracle.

The 12th (City of Sheffield) Battalion ceased to exist in early February 1918 and most of the remaining troops were drafted into the 13th Bn (the 1st Barnsley Pals) or the 7th (Service) Bn, of the York and Lancs Regiment because the army had a severe manpower crisis after the Passchendaele offensive of 1917. During the war around 300 members of the City Battalion applied, and were selected, to become officers, either in their own battalion, or more likely in another regiment. Such a high number was most unusual and underlines the type of recruit the City Battalion attracted.

*Sheffield City Battalion's memorial at Serre*

The sacrifice by the men of the City Battalion has become legend in Sheffield and they are commemorated in the Regimental Chapel in Sheffield Cathedral, at Mark Copse on the old front line at Serre, in Serre village itself, as well as on local school, church and chapel war memorials.

# SGT. ARNOLD LOOSEMORE VC DCM

## Margaret Blenkinsop

Arnold Loosemore was born on the 7th June 1896 at 3 Dyson Lane (now called Dyson Place.) He was one of eight children and like his siblings he attended Clifford Church of England School. After leaving school he was, according to census records, a cowboy; then he became a labourer for a farmer at Whitely Woods. He was living at 1 Lescar Lane, near the Lescar pub when he enlisted in January 1915 aged 19 years and 7 months.

*Private Loosemore in the Duke of Wellington's (West Riding) Regiment*

He joined the York and Lancaster Regiment and was posted to Gallipoli. He survived this campaign and on his return to England was trained as a machine gunner to operate the new Lewis Gun. In 1916 Loosemore was then sent to the Somme to join the 8th Battalion Duke of Wellington (West Riding Regiment).

Arnold Loosemore won the VC on the 11th Aug 1917 at Langemarck, Belgium. His citation reads- *"For most conspicuous bravery and initiative*

*during the attack on a strongly-held enemy position. His platoon having been checked by heavy machine gun fire, he crawled through partially cut wire, dragging his Lewis gun with him, and single-handed dealt with a strong party of the enemy, killing about twenty of them, and thus covering the consolidation of the position taken up by his platoon. Immediately afterwards his Lewis gun was blown up by a bomb, and three enemy soldiers rushed for him, but he shot them all with his revolver. Later, he shot several enemy snipers, exposing himself to heavy fire each time. On returning to the original post he also brought back a wounded comrade under heavy fire at the risk of his life. He displayed throughout an utter disregard of danger."*

This act of bravery led to the award of the VC. He was presented with the VC by George V at Buckingham Palace in January 1918 and by May 1918 he was promoted to Sergeant.

On 19 June 1918 at Zillebeke, Belgium when out with a fighting patrol he displayed conspicuous gallantry and powers of leadership when his officer was wounded and the platoon scattered by hostile bombs. He rallied the men and brought them back in order with all the wounded to our lines. On a subsequent occasion he handled his platoon with great skill and a complete disregard of his own danger under heavy machine gun fire. It was owing to his determination and powers of leadership that the platoon eventually captured the enemy post which they were attacking. He received the Distinguished Conduct Medal for his efforts.

He went back to France and on 13th Oct 1918, 29 days before the Armistice, Arnold was badly wounded in both legs by machine gun fire on a ridge near Villers-en-Cauchies. He eventually had to have one leg amputated and after treatment for his injuries Arnold was discharged in May 1920. On returning to Sheffield on the 24th August he married his childhood sweetheart Amy Morton at St Andrew's Church. They moved to Stannington and the following year had a son, also called Arnold.

*Sergeant Arnold Loose-more shared grave*

*Loosemore heritage building at the Rotary Club site in Castleton*

Despite being disabled and unwell Arnold took up poultry farming but found climbing the stairs of his house exhausting.

In 1923 the Rotary Club provided a wooden bungalow as a home. After his death the hut was dismantled and moved to the Rotary Centre in Castleton where it is used to provide holiday accommodation for school children.

Due to ill health and War wounds, Arnold died of TB on 10th April 1924 at his home. He was 27 years old. His funeral was watched by 1000's who lined the route. The coffin was carried on a gun carriage pulled by 6 horses. The military grandness of the funeral disguised the fact that his widow was destitute. Arnold was buried in a shared grave at All Saints Ecclesall Churchyard.

Despite all he had achieved in the war his widow was refused a war widows pension because she had married him after the war and therefore knew of his ill health. To add insult to injury, his widow was given the bill for his funeral by the City Council. A memorial tablet was placed in St Andrew's Church. When the church was demolished it found its way to Clifford School. The school is very proud of Arnold. Ecclesall Church place poppies on his grave and Sheffield Council named a road in his memory; Loosemore Drive in Gleadless Common. Arnold Loosemore is the only Sheffield man to be awarded the VC who was born and died in the city. The whereabouts of Arnold's medal is unknown. It was sold for £1080 in 1969 and is thought to be in Australia. On the 11th of August 2017, 100 years after winning his VC,

a Commemorative Paving Stone was unveiled at the City War Memorial in Barkers Pool as part of a national scheme to honour the heroes of World War I in their home towns.

*Sergeant Arnold Loosemore paving stone*

## References:

www.chrishobbs.com
www.loosemore.group.shef.ac.uk

# ANYONE FOR TENNIS?
## Susan Gudjonsson

It's over 130 years since tennis was introduced into Nether Edge and in that time there have been five successful Lawn Tennis Clubs (LTC). One by one they have closed down, their courts giving way to the demand for housing land, or their finances falling victim to a dip in enthusiasm for the game. Today only one club, Brentwood LTC, remains. Founded in 1907, the club is proud of its history and in June of 2018 held an Open Day to celebrate the centenary of a very special photograph that hangs on the clubhouse wall. Taken in June 1917, the photo, right, shows tennis players sitting with wounded soldiers, watching a game on Court 3 at Brentwood.

The photograph, taken by Brentwood member Alfred Lucas, came about because in 1915, after tennis players came under criticism for not supporting the war effort, the committee at Brentwood had an idea. They decided to invite wounded soldiers to come to the club once a fortnight during the season to be entertained and to play a game of tennis if they were able. Tea and sandwiches were provided and motorised transport was sent to the local Base Hospital at Collegiate Crescent to collect and return the soldiers. The club offered this hospitality for five seasons, from June 1915 to September 1919. It proved so popular that other local clubs, including Nether Edge Tennis Club (where Birchcroft flats are now) followed Brentwood's example.

So on 25th June this year, Brentwood invited the people of Nether Edge to pay them a visit, as members staged a re-creation of the photograph from 100 years ago. Period costumes were worn, games were played with wooden racquets, while tea and cucumber sandwiches, along with other delicious refreshments, were laid on in the clubhouse. The sun shone, a good time was had by all and at 3 o'clock the old photograph was re-created.

# RUDI WESSELEY, CHILD REFUGEE

## Peter Machan

Rudolph Wessely, always known as 'Rudi', lived with his wife, Wendy, on Montgomery Avenue.  Until he appeared on TV on the Esther Rantzen 'That's Life' programme in 1988 few were aware of his remarkable life story for he had been transported on the last trainload of Jewish children to escape from Prague on the Kindertransport, reaching Liverpool Street station in London, and safety, on 23 August 1939.

Rudi Wessely was just 14 when he said 'farewell' to his parents and left Prague on a specially commissioned train bound for England. He was one of 669 Jewish children rescued from German-occupied Czechoslovakia on the eve of the outbreak of World War Two by Nicholas Winton, the man later dubbed the 'British Schindler'.

After a few days staying in an East End brothel, he made his way to Hull where an Anglican liberal family were offering a home to an unknown Jewish child (and paid the £50 bond to guarantee that the child did not become a burden on the state).

Rudi joined the Royal Navy in late 1943 and worked in intercepting communications from the U-boats as part of a small group of fluent German speakers. He saw action, including D-day on HMS Tartar, and also served on the French ship La Combattante. Speaking in 2016, his son, the eminent psychiatrist Professor Sir Simon Wesseley, said *"my father didn't have a good war. He was sunk twice. Once was terrible (in the North Sea) and he was one of only a few survivors. He had nightmares for all his life about that: the sound of people drowning."* After being demobbed he tried to trace his family, but soon learned from the Red Cross that his parents were dead – his mother murdered at Auschwitz and his father executed at Terezin.

Rudi took British citizenship, studied modern languages at University College, Hull and then trained as a teacher. He stayed in teaching and teacher training for the rest of his professional life.  His first job was at Ecclesfield Grammar in Sheffield, where he met Wendy, a young maths teacher who

*Rudi, with grandsons Ben and Alex and Simon, his son.*

was also a talented violinist and a founder member of the National Youth Orchestra. They married in 1952.

He was also very involved in charitable work, mainly through the Abbeyfield Society, setting up homes for elderly people. In the late 70s he joined the national committee of the Abbeyfield, and there met Sir Nicholas Winton. They worked for the charity for several years, but were unaware of each other's history. Winton's daughter, Barbara, tells the story of what happened next. "They discovered each other in 1983 while both were volunteers for Abbeyfield. Sitting next to each other at a meeting, Nick enquired into Rudi's accent, recognising it as Czech. Rudi talked about his Prague childhood, and Nicholas revealed that he had been in Prague before the war. "Doing what", asked Rudi. "I was running a scheme to get Jewish children into Britain." "Then you are the man that saved my life!" replied Rudi. Nicholas had papers at home with the names of the children who had been brought over, leading to further investigation. Phone calls and letters confirmed Rudi's name was on my father's list and celebrated him finding out at last how he had come to arrive in the UK."

Nick Winton had never before met any of the children he had saved, and now he wanted to meet more. Rudi approached Robert Maxwell, publisher of the Daily Mirror, and with the aid of the Mirror and the episode of 'That's Life', in which there are 40 or so "children" in the audience, the story of the Czech Kindertransport and Winton's part in rescuing more than 600 children emerged. Nicholas Winton was knighted in 2002 and has been honoured in numerous ways by the Czech Government, including a nomination for the 2008 Nobel Peace Prize.

The death of Wendy, his wife, however, left him lonely. His last charitable act was to organise a concert to raise funds for St Luke's, the Sheffield hospice in which Wendy had died. Wendy will be remembered by many local people as she was for many years the senior maths teacher at Brincliffe Grammar School, where, indeed, she attempted to teach me maths! Later she pursued her musical interests. She was instrumental in supporting the development of the City of Sheffield Youth Orchestra and took a post as a violin teacher with Sheffield Music Service and taught my children violin at Carterknowle junior School.

Rudi died aged 88 on Dec 13th 2013. In a Guardian Obituary, His son, Sir Simon Charles Wessely FMedSci, the eminent psychologist who is Professor of Psychological Medicine at the Institute of Psychiatry, King's College London wrote; *"Rudi was a quiet and shy but incredibly kind man, devoted to our mother and latterly to his grandsons. His early experiences made him a natural pessimist, but one who believed in the importance of public service and tolerance. In later life he coped stoically with the progressive loss of his sight."*

---

# REHOUSED IN NETHER EDGE

# Ann Brown

Until the age of four I lived in the centre of Sheffield in a house off the Moor. The Moor was originally common land, which became fields following the enclosures, and then with the growing population in the nineteenth century became built up on both sides in a grid system made up of housing, shops and 'little mesters'.

Throughout World War II we were used to regular air raid sirens, warning and sounding the 'all clear', but one weekend in 1940 there were two major raids on Sheffield, and on December 12th, 1940 we were bombed out of our house

The WRVS and Civil Defence had been preparing for some time for people losing their homes, and had set up centres in schools and church premises. That night we were taken away from the fires to a school centre for shelter. We walked from the Moor, still burning, to my grandmother's house in Totley on the morning after the Blitz and stayed with relatives at Totley for six months until we were re-housed in a shared house at 16 Machon Bank Road, Nether Edge. The local authority had requisitioned empty buildings following the bombing, and they turned this house into two flats. We lived downstairs for the next ten years waiting for a council house! We had a

*16 Machon Bank Road*

front room, which was hardly used, living mainly in the kitchen. This had a Yorkshire range, and a wash-house with a copper. There was a cellar with a stone slab where we kept the meat, butter and milk as there wasn't a fridge. We were given £350 to buy furniture, and the red hawthorn in front of the house is still there!

*Nether Edge shops, 1950s*

My mother had been in service nearby, on the corner of Cherry Tree Road and Meadow Bank Avenue, and was pleased to be able to continue with this daily from our house. I remember she sometimes went to cook lunch for a business man who lived on Sheldon Road when he had visitors. He was called Mr. Little and my mother had grown up with his maid, so she sometimes went to help her friend. Mr. Little belonged to The Bowling Club which was a Gentlemens' club then. He always wore a suit and a gold watch with a chain across his large paunch. Mr. Little enjoyed his whisky every night and lived to be 100.

Our school, St. Wilfrid's R.C. on Queen's Road, Shoreham Street was bombed, so when I started school I went to Broadfield School. Later I went to the Meersbrook Vestry Hall, where our playground was the park! This building was requisitioned for St. Wilfrid's R.C. school to use after the Blitz. When I passed the 11+, I then went to Notre Dame School on Cavendish Street, and from here to Sheffield University and on to teach in Sheffield.

16 Machon Bank Road was close to the shops at Nether Edge, and because it was wartime we had to be registered with a particular shop to buy foods on ration. Fish and vegetables were not on ration, but we bought 'wartime bread' from Grattons, which is now Turners; meat from Tym, the butcher; and sweets from the shop on the corner on Nether Edge

Road  (Sweets were the last thing to come off ration in the early 1950s). There was a Co-op on Sheldon Road.  The grocers had a cashier in the corner who sat behind glass waiting for the canisters containing the cash and bills, to come along wires.  The grocer weighed things like dried fruit or sugar into heavy duty blue bags, and the butter was cut from a block and wrapped in greaseproof paper.  The Co-op also delivered our milk. We would shop every day.  Smith and Hill the chemist was at the far end of the shops on Nether Edge Road. They had glass bottles in the window, and little, labelled drawers on the back wall.  Hay and Son was a 'posh' wine shop, and the post office sold stationery.  In between was a good hardware shop which sold everything, and over the road was a haberdasher. Some of the things Walter Holgate the hardware shop sold include: paraffin for lamps (for the outside toilet), bundles of sticks to light fires, brushes and shovels,  pots and pans, and black lead for the range.

The rag and bone man came round regularly with his horse and cart collecting old clothes and metal.  He sometimes did not give any money,  but would exchange things for donkey stone which we used on the edge of the steps.  The coal man delivered the coal with his horse and cart, and would carry the heavy bags up the steps.  A knife sharpener came round too.

The old tram shed over the road  was where American army trucks came to be serviced or repaired.  I had never seen black Americans before, and remember them queueing all the way up the road outside our house waiting for their turn.  They gave me chewing gum and real coffee. I also remember there was a barrage balloon on the tennis courts on the corner of Glen Road and Ashland Road.

We had spent Christmas 1940 at Totley with my Grandmother, having lost everything in the fires that destroyed our home. My mother talked about the Christmas puddings she had made which were lost, but Christmas was celebrated as well as possible in Sheffield, the pantomimes took place as usual, the theatres escaped the damage.  By Christmas 1941 we were rehoused in Nether Edge. With rationing the usual cakes and poultry were impossible, people had to improvise and my mother who had been a cook in private households was not very good at this and gave up the battle. I remember liquid paraffin which was a medicine was used to make pastry and there were plenty of cook books and Ministry of Food leaflets to help housewives. My father was Irish and our relations in Ireland sent us butter wrapped in leaves and unbelievably we had trays of eggs arrive unbroken.

At Christmas my aunt sent chickens with their innards and feathers complete. My mother was used to gutting and plucking poultry but the smell was awful. The chicken tasted good. One of my aunts lived in Grindleford and reared a pig which was killed at Christmas and we all expected a share in the meat. Other members of the family had chickens, so eggs were available for cooking, dried egg was useful as well. I can remember turning a glass jar with cream from the top of the milk to make butter. When things improved we had goose rather than turkey, there was a lot of fat to deal with and all cooking was in the oven of a Yorkshire range and a tiny gas ring.

Christmas decorations were paper chains and nothing new during the war. Family parties were held at one of my aunts' houses and a walk home in the blackout, the buses did not run on Christmas day. We played card games and two of my uncles dressed up as Gert and Daisy, a popular radio comedy act. Another uncle did conjuring tricks, not very well.  At school we did a Nativity play and other concert performances. Carol concerts and Midnight Mass when I was a bit older were at church. Our Christmas stockings always had an orange when available and new money. I remember an Enid Blyton Book. Christmas was celebrated as much as was possible, and children were sheltered from the harsh realities of wartime especially at Christmas.

I was an only child so was often sent out on errands, sometimes for "Woodbines", and on Saturdays for tripe.  I would go on the tram along Abbeydale Road to the bottom of Carterknowle Road to the tripe shop, and we would have this either hot with onions and milk, or cold with vinegar and salt.  We regularly went to the Abbeydale Cinema House. There was a chip shop on Abbeydale Road, and as a treat on Friday after Church Club we would have a 'pennorth and scraps'.

Because the Catholic Church had been bombed, we went to Mass in the cinema on Abbeydale Road

*Ann Brown and herself as a child*

and then later, St. Peter's, Machon Bank. The presbytery was on the corner of Machon Bank and Moncrieffe Road and three priests and their housekeeper lived there. The neighbours were not happy as there was quite a bit of anti-Catholic feeling, but we enjoyed playing in the garden, and going to garden parties there.

I had a lot of friends in Nether Edge, playing in houses around, and up the hill at Brincliffe Edge woods and allotments, but when I was 15 we decided to take a council house at Longley which we had been offered. Sadly, my father died soon after this, but my mother stayed there for the rest of her life. I lived there until I was married in 1961.

# Part 5

# Activists

*Suffragettes March*

# VOTES FOR WOMEN, The Suffrage Campaign in Sheffield & Nether Edge.

## Ruth Bernard

A hundred years ago on the 6th February 2018, six million women who were householders over the age of 30 were given the vote. This was the result of a long campaign by the Women's Social and Political Union (WSPU), the National Union of Women's Suffrage Societies (NUWSS) and others. Although much of the history of the campaign has centred on its leading figures in Manchester and London, Sheffield had a very active suffragette movement; in fact it was the first place to form a women's suffrage society run by women for women.

### The Sheffield Women's Political Association 1851

On 26th February 1851 the Sheffield Women's Political Association (SWPA) held its inaugural meeting at the Temperance Hotel in Queen Street. Anne Knight delivered 'An Address to the Women of England', encouraging them to unite and claim their political rights. The Association produced the first Suffrage Manifesto, submitted a petition to the House of Lords and received support from all over England and from France. It would however be another 50 years before the suffrage movement really gained momentum.

### Suffragists and Suffragettes

In 1897 the National Union of Women's Suffrage Societies (NUWSS) was founded; its members were known as suffragists. The Sheffield branch was run by Dr Helen Wilson, a doctor of medicine. She was born in Mansfield and trained at the London School of Medicine. Her Father was the Liberal MP for Holmfirth. The approach of the NUWSS was to achieve change through influencing and peaceful campaigning. In Nether Edge, Dr Wilson's work was supported by Louise and Mary Gledstone, wife and daughter of James Gledstone, minister of Abbeydale Road Congregational Church. They lived at 42 Crescent Road and were President and Secretary of the Sheffield Women's Suffrage Society but both women left Sheffield in 1907 following the death of James Gledstone.

Six years later, in 1903, the Women's Social & Political Union (WSPU) was founded by Emmeline Pankhurst in Manchester, as a breakaway society prepared to adopt a more assertive approach. Initially a small pressure group within the Independent Labour Party, the members of the WSPU adopted the name suffragettes. Emmeline and her daughters Christabel and Sylvia were all involved. Youngest daughter Adela was only 18 in 1903 but she would later play an important role in the suffrage campaign in Sheffield.

Several suffrage bills were presented in parliament in the late 19th century, but all failed. The WSPU changed tactics and their campaign became more militant. As a result of direct action, members were arrested, many were sent to prison (where some went on hunger strike) and in 1913 Emily Davison was fatally injured at the Derby when she ran in front of the King's horse.

## The Campaign Gathers Momentum in Sheffield

Sheffield women continued to be very active in the campaign; one of those involved was Edith Whitworth, born in Aston in 1870. She married a postal telegraphist in 1893 and moved to Nether Edge, living at 70 Wath Road, where the couple had two children.

In 1903 Christabel Pankhurst, of the WSPU and Isabella Fox of the NUWSS, spoke at the Cemetery Road Vestry Hall urging women to join the cause. (The hall is located just outside Waitrose; it is now the Somali Community Association). Edith Whitworth was on the platform and was the mover of a resolution demanding immediate legislation extending the franchise to women. The Sheffield branch of the WSPU was founded in 1906, with Edith Whitworth as its Secretary, and the inaugural meeting was held at her house in Wath Road.

*Edith Whitworth 1907*

On 13th Feb 1907 Edith, along with 3 other suffragettes, was arrested outside the House of Commons and spent 14 days in Holloway prison. She was described as one of the most enthusiastic disciples of the WSPU. In court she said she had a mission; *"I want the vote to help the poor and starving children. I believe that will be the lever by which sweated women will be able to help themselves".* (Sheffield Evening Telegraph 14.2.1907)

She was friends with Adela Pankhurst, daughter of Emmeline Pankhurst. Adela lived in Broomhill for two years and was very active in working for the WSPU in Yorkshire. In 1908 Reginald McKenna, First Lord of the Admiralty,

*The Vestry Hall, Cemetery Road*

was due to speak at the Cutlers' Hall. Adela, Edith and other suffragettes, disguised themselves as kitchen maids to gain entrance to the Cutlers' Hall and disrupt the meeting. The police guarding the entrance made this impossible so the women went to the Town Hall and Adela addressed the crowd of 8-900 people. Many of those present were unemployed hunger marchers and they cheered Adela and then marched with her back to the Cutlers' Hall. A scuffle ensued involving the police and the hunger strikers; Adela and Edith were also caught up in the fracas. They retreated, Adela changed her clothes and returned but they were recognised and were roughly escorted away.

## A Third Suffrage Organisation

The WSPU was becoming more militant and Edith began to feel concerned about these tactics. Much to Adela's dismay, she joined the breakaway Women's Freedom League (WFL), which had a small branch in Sheffield and favoured non-violent forms of protest. The WFL was founded in 1908, and continued with peaceful forms of protest such as non-payment of taxes and organising demonstrations. Adela carried on the fight in Sheffield but, with increasing risks of imprisonment, support began to drift away. Dr Helen Wilson was outraged by the undignified 'kitchen maid' tactics used at the Cutlers' Hall demonstration. In response she attended a rally in Manchester, wearing her doctoral cap and gown and carrying a large NUWSS banner embroidered in silk and bearing the slogan, 'Sheffield Demands Votes for Women'. It epitomised the divide between the two sides of the suffrage movement.

## Political Change in Sheffield

In 1909 a political crisis led to important changes in Sheffield. Lloyd George's 'Peoples' Budget' bill had been rejected and shortly afterwards the Liberal MP for Attercliffe died, triggering a by-election. Helen Wilson campaigned peacefully for the NUWSS, urging voters to sign an Electors' Petition. Adela Pankhurst led the campaign for the WSPU against the Liberal candidate, holding dozens of meetings. The WFL ran its own meetings and its supporters signed suffrage postcards, which they sent to Asquith. Labour won and the Liberals were defeated; the new MP took 5000 suffrage signatures with him to London later that summer.

In the same year, women imprisoned for their suffrage activity began hunger strikes and some WSPU suffragettes stepped up their direct action campaigns. Activist Molly Morris came from Lancashire to run the WSPU shop in Chapel Walk, selling goods and pamphlets to raise funds. Ella Schuster, who had spent time in prison for protesting and stone-throwing, worked alongside her. At night they chalked suffrage slogans near factories and sabotaged post boxes with ink and improvised explosives.

Adela continued to work for the WSPU until Autumn 1911, although she became increasingly disillusioned with its violent tactics. By then her health was failing, her younger brother Harry had died and she was repeatedly being criticised by her mother Emmeline and sisters, Christabel and Sylvia. They had moved further to the right politically while she was supporting socialism. Ostracized by her family, Adela left England for Australia in February 1914, on a one-way passage funded by her Mother. Fortunately she found happiness there, marrying socialist widower Tom Walsh, raising a family of eight children and working as a journalist and speaker for the Women's Political Association.

*Adela Pankhurst, 1908*

**Women's Place in Sheffield Politics since 1918.**

In the period before the First World War Liberal Prime Minister Asquith blocked all attempts to introduce female suffrage reform but change could not be resisted once war was over. In February 1918 women householders over 30 did gain the vote and all women over 21 were finally enfranchised in 1928, ten years later than men. Coincidentally this was also the year in which Emmeline Pankhurst died. In Sheffield in 1919 Eleanor Barton became the first woman to be elected to the City Council. The first female mayor, Ann Longden, was appointed in 1936 and Joan Maynard became the first female MP for Sheffield in 1974. Currently (in 2018), 29 of the city's 84 councillors and 3 of the 6 MPs representing Sheffield are women.

**Sources:** Jill Liddington  'Rebel Girls', Virago, 2006, London
Sheffield Evening Telegraph, 14th February 1907
'Sources for the Study of Women's Suffrage' Sheffield Archives and Local Studies Library.    Thanks to John Baxendale for his contribution.

# AMY JOHNSON IN SHEFFIELD

# Paul Steele

A rainy day in Bridlington would seem an unlikely place to start a tale about one of the Twentieth Century's most inspirational women. Nonetheless this is where I stumbled across the connection that linked Amy Johnson (1903-1941), the world famous aviatrix and first female pilot to fly solo to Australia, to the leafy suburbs of Sheffield. Looking for somewhere dry to take the family we happened upon Sewerby Hall on Bridlington's north coast. It was there that an exhibition about the life and times of the famous flyer, was displaying an array of her personal items. Amid these was a framed letter to a friend, signed off from 3 Grange Crescent Road. For those unfamiliar, this is one of the large

Victorian terraced villas off Cemetery Road. Indeed the front door is barely 10 yards from the upper entrance to the General Cemetery.

After some research, aided by the University of Sheffield Archivist, I was able to confirm that this was the abode of Amy for the duration of her 3 year tenure while undertaking a degree. Born in Hull in 1903, the eldest of 4 girls to a family connected to the fishing industry, she was one of the first women to be accepted into the University of Sheffield, graduating with a Bachelor of Arts in Economics in 1925.

If this seemed pioneering for its time, it was small beer compared to her achievements over the next 2 decades. A love affair took her to London, where she became interested in flying, having taken a bus in an idle moment to Stag Lane Aerodrome in North London. She was hooked, and continued to spend most of her spare time at the Aerodrome. Supporting her passion for flight she worked as a secretary and received assistance from her father to enable her to gain the qualifications to become a pilot. Not one to do things by half measures, in 1929 she also gained qualifications as an aero mechanic

and became the first woman to obtain a Ground Engineer's C Licence - skills she would put to good use in her coming adventures.

The purchase of a Gypsy Moth plane soon followed. It was in this contraption, named Jason, she set off from Croydon on May 5th 1930. Arriving on May 24th in Australia's Northern Territory, she received a rapturous reception from a huge crowd gathered to witness the historic event. An incredible feat in what was essentially a wood and canvas framed plane that was even at the time outdated technology. To top it all she crashed on her arrival in Darwin. Mostly unscathed she went on to achieve further worldwide fame in the 1930's for her completion of many other long distance flights, often setting time records to boot.

She worked for the Air Transport Auxiliary during the Second World War but sadly lost her life on January 5th 1941. Mystery surrounds the cause of her crash into the Thames Estuary. Some speculate it was bad weather, others think it was the result of "friendly fire". None the less she perished transporting an RAF aircraft from Blackpool to Kidlington airbase in Oxfordshire. She was certainly well off course. The flight should have taken 90 minutes, but after over four hours her plane ditched, 100 miles off course and 12 mile off the coast of Herne Bay. Although spotted in the water by a nearby boat who tried to rescue her, her body was never recovered.

She crammed a lot into her short life, and it is nice to think that Sheffield was formative in the moulding of this remarkable woman in some small part. She could have wandered down Psalter Lane, popped into The Stag for a drink with friends. Who knows? Nonetheless it is fun to imagine her in our patch. If you do get the time I heartily recommend you search online

for footage of her trip to Australia. It is fantastic to see Amy's arrival and interview. She was truly a woman ahead of her time and an inspiration to others.

*Amy in the cockpit on her last flight.*

# MARY WALLY TYZACK, GIRL GUIDE LEADER
## Nick Waite

Miss Tyzack, as she was always known, is the only one of the Nether Edge Tyzacks still remembered by the older and former residents who contributed to this short account of her life. In the absence of personal documentation we have to rely on the memories of those who had personal knowledge of a uniquely memorable character.

Before the Great War, her father Stuart Meggitt Tyzack spent some time in France, then a new market for the products of W Tyzack Sons and Turner. Stuart was the great great grandson of the company's founder William and he would later become joint Managing Director with his brother, also called William. In his early twenties Stuart married a German woman, Auguste Meizer. They were still in France when Mary was born in 1908 and her only brother Wilfred in 1909.

By 1911 the young family, with a German nanny, had returned to 244 Carterknowle Road, not in Nether Edge but equally convenient for both the Abbeydale and Little London Works. In 1921, Mary's grandfather Stuart Tyzack senior died, and her parents then moved into the fine house and grounds at 7 Williamson Road, which had been the family home since it was built in 1890; Mary lived there for the rest of her long life.

For young women of that era, born into relative wealth and a conventional background, expectations were limited; a good marriage, voluntary work and a sparkling social life. Only a few were active in the management of family businesses or achieved professional independence. Mary never married or worked in the family firm. It is known that after 1945 she was active in the Girl Guides but research for this piece by the Sheffield Guides' archivist showed that this dated from 1929 when, aged 21, she became Captain of

the 17th Sheffield (St Andrew's Sharrow) Guides and by 1931 was also Captain of Sharrow Rangers. It was then that she began to lead her Guides on the annual camps to destinations including Robin Hood's Bay, Filey

*Lacrosse Team;*
*Mary (bottom right) seated next to Joan*

*Mary (right) during her time with the Mechanised Transport Corps.*

and Grange over Sands in Cumbria.

During the pre-war period she shared a social life with her cousins Brian, Peter and Joan, as described in the article on Sharrow Bank. She was especially close to Joan, some 10 years younger; at the time Mary was Captain of the senior Guides, Joan was Tawney Owl of the St Andrew's Brownies. In 1936 William Tyzack and his family moved to Belsize Road in Fulwood, which may explain one informant's suggestion that Mary was a leader of the Nether Green Guides in the late 1930s. The family photograph shows Mary and Joan in the same Sheffield lacrosse team.

As with many young middle class women, it was the 1939-45 War which gave Mary a new role, as a lorry driver with the Mechanised Transport Corps, the equivalent of the better known women who flew war planes from factories to airfields all over Britain. This was exhausting, challenging but valuable work which she later told her Girl Guide members was a great experience; she particularly remembered getting so tired that she learned to cat nap at the roadside, sitting on a kerb and leaning against a cold stone wall, waiting outside headquarters for the next assignment.

After 1945, it was back to the comfortable life in Williamson Road, and the start of 20 more years' involvement with the Girl Guides of St Andrew's and the wider world which illuminated the extraordinary personality still so well remembered 27 years after her death. Personal memories relate to her time with the St Andrew's groups, but the archives reveal her involvement with national and international aspects of Guiding. As Division Commander for Sheffield East from 1945 to 1954, she led the first group of Sheffield Guides to the movement's international centre ("Our Chalet") at Adelboden in Switzerland. In the same year (1947) she was involved in a large rally in the grounds of Endcliffe Hall – doubtless with sisterly persuasion, because the records show the event was "by kind permission of Col. W Tyzack". Two years later, and again with her brother's "kind permission", there was a reception at Endcliffe Hall to welcome the Chief Guide, Olive Baden-Powell on her first visit to Sheffield. In those years Mary also attended an international camp in Finland and welcomed visiting Guide dignitaries from the USA,

Finland, Switzerland, Sweden and Luxemburg. Some were invited to stay in Williamson Road, for instance in 1959 a Mrs Dutt, the International Commissioner for India. In consequence of all these activities she became a representative on the Sheffield Standing Conference on Voluntary Organisations.

So much for her responsibilities within the wider movement, but what was Mary like as a person and why so clearly and fondly remembered in Nether Edge? I only met her briefly on two occasions and as a non-churchgoer know little of her involvement in the worship, service and parochial business of St Andrew's, but I have been fortunate to correspond with or meet a large number of former Guides on whose vivid recollections this central section of her story is based.

Those informants and others confirm her manner could be abrasive and outspoken; she brooked no argument when her mind was settled, as it usually was; socially a little arrogant, self-willed, demanding the highest standards of dress, behaviour and achievement, never suffering fools gladly, a bit of a tyrant in her governance of the girls - someone of whom many "felt in awe". And yet she was endlessly kind, supportive and thoughtful, a woman who wanted and obtained only the best from the girls and from herself - a mixture of the forbidding and the caring, a memory from a half century ago of what one informant still calls "the most dynamic woman I have met". Another said, "she had a huge influence on me" and a third that, after almost 50 years, she still relies on the moral lessons instilled in those few years. Involvement with her was enormous fun – to everyone in Nether Edge, she was "Miss Tyzack" but former Guides confirm she was always known to them as "Tizzie". As another wrote to me "she just knew instinctively what was exciting and fun for youngsters.... we adored her and were in awe of her in equal measure". Another informant who knew her in later years described her as "a formidable figure, very kind really but very strict....it was the old school, appearance was more important than kindly commitment".

The accounts of the annual camp are typical - in later years near Birchover in Derbyshire, at Brodsworth Hall near Doncaster, or once as far as Brightlingsea in

*7 Williamson Road*

Essex. One correspondent described "packing a huge coach outside her house with tents, bedding racks, washing up stands and tripods (gadgets she'd made in advance in her garden), campfire bricks and grids, food, pots and pans to feed 35 or so, toilets and loo tents, wash tents, a roof for the camp fire, personal gear.....Camp had strict rules but patrol leaders were allowed to invite any Scouts they could find to visit for a camp fire in the evenings. The singing at camp was fantastic; I don't think Tizzie sang, but she enjoyed it, and sometimes wasn't keen if the words got a bit silly or suggestive".  Another informant said the coach dated from the interwar period, chosen by Tizzie to keep a traditional feel to the expedition; yet another remembered a slightly earlier time when everyone travelled in a furniture van surrounded by military style kitbags.

Some detail may be apocryphal but not the overall impression of Williamson Road, unchanged in appearance, furnishings or décor since it was built in 1890.  The Guides had their regular Friday evening meetings there, described as "running like clockwork, with plenty to do and learn, with complete discipline; the nearest to army life I've ever come". There was a large lawn behind the house where they could practice erecting tents or making gadgets for the camps – but if it rained, they went inside. The house itself was always dark with a particular smell, which the older guides said was because Tizzie was a "secret gin drinker which gave her a thrilling naughtiness".  Was this apocryphal like the vintage coach?  No, and  not really a secret either; the family confirm that, as was common amongst the well-to-do middle classes of the early 20th century, gin and assorted cocktails were the daily lubricants of social life.  It shocked me when one Guide from the 1950s, said "you could smell the alcohol on her breath at any time from morning to night", but family informants were not surprised when I repeated this, and it was borne out by the tale of another former Guide on her first camp, walking up the field when everyone was supposed to be in tents for the night, seeing Tizzie through the thin canvas of her own tent pouring herself a stiff gin.  Nobody ever suggested that the habit in any way it affected her duties as Guide leader.

It all fits with the young girls' impressions of life in the unnerving candlelit big house. At that impressionable age, architectural details might have escaped them, but the sense of a former age was unmistakeable.  Apart from the regular Friday evenings, they were sometimes asked (or summoned) to small parties, especially when recently promoted from the Brownies. The house rarely seemed to be fully lit, often just by candles, but

*Mary at a family party in the 1980s* how welcoming and exciting Tizzie could be, playing "murder" amongst the drapes and curtains. As one wrote to me "it was a very spooky house" and added *"it had curtains swathed across the arch at the top of the very gracious stairs so that as soon as you entered the house you felt you were in an Adams Family set or a ghost train".* Those who lived near Williamson Road might be dragooned into caring for the plants in the large conservatory during Tizzie's absences, a "nerve wracking experience" because of the volume of detailed written instructions, but again a *"wonderful encounter with a world gone by….an Edwardian world full of palms and exotics".*

Even after she resigned as leader of the St Andrew's Guides in about 1968, Mary remained a forthright and significant figure within the Sheffield Guides, with particular reference to their Outdoor Centre in the remaining outbuildings of Whiteley Wood Hall (the main house was demolished in 1959). In honour of "all she did for the Centre and her many years in the cause of Guiding, one of the "cottages" which provide accommodation for Guides at the Centre is named after her. Nonetheless it is her 20 or so years of practical leadership in Nether Edge which exemplifies the unique character by which she is now remembered, indeed venerated, by many of those who came directly under her influence

In her eccentricity she reflected the extraordinary house in which she lived, alone after her parents' deaths and Wilfred's move to Kingfield Road after his marriage. Readers who have visited the National Trust's "Mr Straw's House" in Worksop will know it as a time capsule of middle class life, untouched by modernisation or "improvement" for nearly a century, and Williamson Road was the same, just much bigger. Visitors in Mary's later years remember this well, because by then the house had another parochial purpose. When in the late sixties the St Andrew's Church Garden Party lost its home in Sharrowvale Road, Mary offered the garden of 7 Williamson Road, still substantial despite an earlier sale of part of it for housing on Clifford Road. For many years until her death this was a notable Nether Edge event, conveniently situated almost opposite the church which, perhaps fortunately for her peace of mind, was not demolished until after her death. Like many residents, I recall the shock of walking into a time warp of late Victorian life.

The room which struck me most forcibly was described by a more frequent visitor as "a superb example of a Victorian or Edwardian billiards room with a magnificent table, all the necessary cue racks and scoreboards and upholstered seating".   Mary used to permit the Scouts, and earlier even some of the Guides, to use the table, and "loved to see it used and appreciated".   She also allowed the Guides and others to prepare refreshments in the sequence of two or three kitchens including scullery and sluice room – but woe betide anyone who used the wrong one for any other than its assigned purpose

To the end of her life, family and visitors confirm she remained as forthright, eccentric and  independent as in the Guiding years.  Social life continued unabated; each year she held a Twelfth Night Party to which twelve guests were always invited; and after the dinner, the men were despatched to the Billiard Room to entertain themselves. She continued to delight the family's young children, hiding Easter eggs all over the garden, many undiscovered for months, and she made elaborate stuffed toys for them and for sale at the Garden Parties. From time to time she would travel for anything up to a month to visit her mother's family in Germany, and one relative told me she would be speaking fluent German on her return. Perhaps unsurprisingly she had a succession of pairs of dachshunds, described to me as "feral" and fed on a diet of raw mince; she could sometimes be heard in local woods, shouting their unusual names to call them to heel.

In her eighties she broke her arm falling out of an apple tree picking fruit for her endless jars of chutney, and when a friend asked for the recipe she refused, unless he came to pick the fruit with her.  To the end she lived frugally, though whether through financial necessity or choice is unclear. By her last years, the family company was much less successful than in its heyday when many Tyzacks lived in large houses in Nether Edge with servants to cushion their everyday lives. Her second cousin told me he found her painting the billiard room ceiling the day before she died, according to him because she didn't believe in paying decorators.

## Resources

 See also;- 'The Tyzacks in Nether Edge' and 'Sharrow Bank' featured in this book.    Sheffield Central Library, Local Studies Department.

Personal memories or information from : Liz Birkby, Katherine Clark, Penny Dyer, Marilyn Godber, Brian Hiscoe, Ann Hutton, Nick Hutton, Thilde Lowe, Julie MacDonald (the Guides archivist), Diana Rayner, Chris Venables and special thanks to Martin Greenshields

# MOHAMMED NAZIR, COMMUNITY ACTIVIST
## David Price

Nether Edge today is one of the more cosmopolitan parts of Sheffield. Its biggest ethnic minority is of course the Pakistanis and this community includes many notable characters. I describe here one of the community's elder statesmen – Haji Mohammed Nazir OBE. He has lived in Sheldon Road since 1974. The word Haji means that he has made a pilgrimage to Mecca; his Muslim faith has been important throughout his life. His OBE was awarded in 1998 for his extensive service to the community.

As with many Asian immigrants, Nazir's move to Britain was linked with the British Empire and the two World Wars. Nazir was born in 1931 in Rawalpindi in what was then British India. He came from a military family. His father had fought in both World Wars. In the First World War, he fought in France and was wounded and taken to the UK a few days before his entire platoon was wiped out, He was given 25 acres of farmland by the Indian Government. In the Second World War, his former major contacted him as an experienced 'Subedar' (a high ranking Indian in the Indian Army) and he rejoined the Indian Army. He became a lieutenant and was given a medal (OBI or Order of British India).

In 1947, when Nazir was still at school in Rawalpindi, the city became part of the new state of Pakistan when India was partitioned. Nazir describes what happened at the time of partition as 'very cruel' and 'disgusting'. There were dramatic movements of people and terrible massacres. Nazir recalls a Hindu boy at his school with whom he was friendly, but partition seemed to turn Hindus into enemies.

Nazir went to the University of the Punjab in Lahore and in 1953 obtained his BA. In 1955 he started work as a teacher. He later obtained a BEd and went back to teaching in a secondary school. His move to the UK in 1964 was reluctant. He says: 'I did not really want to go to England', but the fact that he had relations and friends in Sheffield and Glasgow encouraged him to try out the UK, hoping to continue his career as a teacher here. He also says that the present Queen in a speech at that time encouraged people with a military background from the Indian sub-continent to come to Britain.

Arriving in England, he found it difficult to decide whether to stay in Glasgow or in Sheffield, but was eventually persuaded by his Sheffield friends to stay with them in Attercliffe. He found it impossible to become a teacher, so he got a job briefly in a steel company and then worked as a railway shunter – which was hard. After a year, the marshalling yard closed and he became a bus conductor and then a bus driver. He passed an Institute of Transport exam and applied to be an Inspector, but was turned down. He says ruefully: 'They were not taking black people.'

He then became a taxi driver, at a time when there were not many Pakistani taxi drivers. He also became increasingly involved as a voluntary adviser, helping members of his community with paper work, passport forms, immigration applications etc, as he was educated and many of them were not. He became Secretary of the Asian Welfare Association (AWA), which Akhtar Kayani, a former businessman, had founded in Sharrow.

By 1974, the house that he had acquired in Staniforth Road was due for demolition, so he bought his present house in Sheldon Road and became part of the growing Pakistani community in Nether Edge. By 1979-80, he was so highly motivated in his voluntary advisory work that he applied successfully for a paid job as an advice worker in an ethnic minorities advice project in Spital Lane. Then from 1980-95 he was a tutor/lecturer to unemployed people in Darnall (an outlying centre of Castle College, later, Sheffield College). At this stage in his life, he was very absorbed in education. He was for a short time a Governor of Abbeydale Grange School and he recalls going there with Julian Sullivan, Vicar of St Mary's, Bramall Lane, to talk to the students at morning assembly about Islam and Christianity. He was also Governor of various local primary schools, such as Sharrow Junior and Lowfield, where he gave similar talks.

Islam has always played a major part in Nazir's life - he was always 'religious -minded'. Arriving in Nether Edge, he was concerned that there was no mosque in the area. He recalls that during Ramadan Muslims used to meet at Mount Pleasant in Sharrow, but the friendly caretaker would want to turn them out before they had finished their prayers. He and his colleagues held a meeting of the

*The Co-op in Wolseley Road used as a mosque*

community at the Star of Asia and set up a Trust with him as Chair of Trustees.

In 1982, they bought a former Co-op store in Wolseley Road. There was some concern among local residents that there would be a lot of noise from the banging of drums, but a Methodist Minister, John Peadon, who ran the South Sheffield Project, helped to persuade local people that this was not the case. Nazir and his colleagues converted one floor into a mosque for worship and another floor into a day centre for the elderly. But the community was growing and these premises were not large enough. So they explored various options for a new mosque, including Abbeydale Cinema (which for a time they owned) and St Peter's Church. Eventually, they decided to demolish the Co-op store building and to build a brand new mosque in its place in Wolseley Road. A great deal of fund raising took place. In 2003 construction work began and by 2005 the grand and impressive Madina Mosque had been built in Wolseley Road. It cost £5 million.

As the Pakistani community became more established in Sheffield, Nazir became concerned at his compatriots' difficulties in dealing with death in the family. They did not understand British regulations on the action to take when a loved one died and they did not know how to observe Muslim burial rites in a Sheffield context. He set up a committee to help people. This has now developed into a funeral society, which is also a mutual society, helping to pay for funeral costs. Alongside all these religious concerns, Nazir was also very active politically. He had been a member of the Labour Party since the 1970s. He says that Richard Caborn helped him a lot. In 1995, he was persuaded to stand for the Council in Sharrow and he became a Councillor. A year later, in order to enable him to spend more time on Council work, he applied for early retirement from the College. He served on police community liaison panels. He became among other things Vice Chair of the South Yorkshire Fire Authority. He found himself attending many meetings, which was tiring. He recalls coming back home at 9 pm one evening after meetings all day and finding someone who wanted him to do 4 or 5 passport applications. He did not turn them way but spent the next two hours filling in

*Madina Mosque in Wolseley Road*

the forms. He felt a religious duty to help others. He left the Council in 2004 following boundary changes.

From 1968 onwards, he was a member of the Sheffield Racial Equality Council, which had been set up under Government legislation to combat discrimination and promote racial equality. He worked closely with Debjani Chatterjee, who was a very pro-active Community Relations Officer from 1984 onwards. Later on, he became Chair of SREC. He was very disappointed when in 2010 SREC had to close down owing to lack of funding.

For many decades, Nazir's life was frenetically busy. He is appreciative of the support and patience of his first wife who sadly died in 1999. He has four sons and one daughter and many grandchildren and great grand children. More recently, he has remarried.

Nazir is now 87 and less active than he was in earlier years, though still lively and vigorous. He remains Chair of the Trustees of Madina Mosque, even if the day to day running of the Mosque is delegated to a Management Committee. He is still involved in the funeral society which he founded. He can look back on remarkable achievements both in supporting his community and in helping to integrate his community into Sheffield life. It is no wonder that he was awarded the OBE in 1998. He is glad that he settled in Sheffield, which he describes as a peaceful friendly place where communities get on well with each other.

---

# ROBERT SPOONER

## Elizabeth Birks

Robert Spooner studied civil engineering at King's College London and retired a few years ago as a professional engineer (working on projects in the UK like Twickenham Rugby Ground, the Jodrell Bank Telescope as well as a short-term project in Mexico), but he is better known locally not just as a white-bearded man who wears sandals and cycles nearly everywhere, but for walking, singing, leading choirs, art facilitating, gardening, jam-making, preaching with the Methodist Church, and speaking about poverty issues and about those seeking asylum.

He was born in Manchester in 1939 to parents who were fanatical about

grand opera. They both sang. Robert sang. As a child he had to wave a fan behind Dido. Later, he was tasked with carrying a letter to Violetta in La Traviata on stage but he forgot something – the letter for the letter aria! He was a principal singer with South Yorkshire Opera and sang in 40 operas in toto, as well as oratorios. He currently conducts the University of the Third Age (U3A) choir called 'Vintage Voices' which performs for older people in care homes, lunch clubs and similar venues.

One day his wife Margaret was asked by Myra Davis if she could suggest a Chair for the meeting to be held that evening to discuss what could be done to help those asylum seekers who were facing destitution. Margaret said: 'My husband will Chair it for tonight only'. He had by then been involved with the 'Sunday Centre' and 'Archer Project' and was currently Chair of 'Homeless and Rootless at Christmas' (HARC). He chaired the first ever meeting of the group setting up Asylum Seeker Support Initiative – Short Term (ASSIST) and never looked back. Robert is no longer the Chair but ASSIST is now supporting 100 people with money and is able to offer over 40 places to sleep. It has 6 employees and loads of volunteers and only latterly has seen the amount of income coming from grants exceeding the money being donated by local people. Robert has helped groups beyond Sheffield to set up support structures to help refugees and asylum seekers, such as Doncaster Conversation Club.

Robert these days is usually found helping at the ASSIST stalls in the garden on the corner of Glen Road at Nether Edge Farmers' Market, worshipping with Nether Edge Quakers, singing with the Sterndale Singers and leading Vintage Voices. He's still out and about raising awareness about refugee issues. His driving force is his concern for people who are poor. He hates seeing beggars in the street and says they weren't around in the 1970s. He wants to be part of an 'equal opportunity society' where the poor are helped and the rich have concern for the poor. He feels if inequality could be lessened that would increase everyone's happiness.

# MYRA DAVIS

## Elizabeth Birks

When I arrived back in Sheffield in the year 2000, I came to live in Nether Edge and I kept bumping into an intense white-haired woman who got me involved in what she was doing. 'How about helping to sew costumes for the Merlin Theatre? Come in and see the fabulous costume currently in the sewing machine.' 'Would you like to help recce a walk in Derbyshire for U3A?' 'Oh! Fancy seeing you at REEP (Refugee Education and Employment Project). Would you like to come for tea as I've invited some REEP students round?'

*Myra Davis (née Palmer) 1938 - 2014)*

At a 'Stop the War' teach-in we were organising a workshop on refugee issues and this gave rise to the *Sheffield Refugee Friendship Group* and then to *Sheffield Conversation Club*. But conversation does not keep the wolf from the door and something more substantial was needed for those asylum seekers with no food and no place to stay. Organisations like CDAS (Committee for the Defence of Asylum Seekers) and NRC (Northern Refugee Centre) were supportive in the setting up of ASSIST (Asylum Seeker Support Initiative – Short Term) and what started in Myra's front room, soon became a vibrant charity with loads of projects and volunteers and lots of host families offering destitute asylum seekers a bed or a sofa for a night or a few days or even weeks. Myra was one such host and was not just providing somewhere to sleep but she was also acting as a surrogate mum or gran to many, many individuals and couples. She wouldn't give in. If someone asked for help, she'd do what she could to help. I wonder how many MPs dedicated their time to helping Myra's protégés.

It's strange that she talked very little about her life in the last century. Her daughter, Ali, wrote an article published in the 2014 memorial edition of Sheffield Conversation Club newsletter and said that Myra had an MA in South African Theatre and that when Ali was little, she spent time baking cakes for Amnesty International fundraisers. In that edition, so many asylum seekers and refugees spoke so warmly of this amazing woman. Does her memory deserve a blue plaque?

# Part 6
# Streets & Houses

*Kenwood Lodge*

# THEY LIVED ON PSALTER LANE
# Ruth A. Morgan

Psalter Lane, a ridge road extending west out of Sheffield, was once an ancient salt route across Sharrow Moor, a rough track where 'snuff mill' owner William Wilson shot grouse in 1796. In 1758 it became part of the turnpike road to Chapel-en-le-Frith until 1812 when Ecclesall Road was made. The Stag Hotel, built in 1805, once included rear stabling for 24 horses and two carriages for travellers' use. As development gathered pace in the 1850s, the road was widened and surfaced, and later trees were planted.

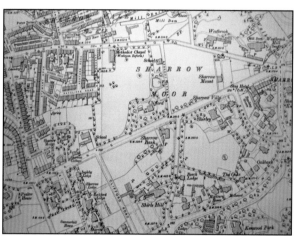

Fields on either side became building plots for the stone villas and terraced houses we see today. The three Wilson brothers who developed the snuff business in the valley, Joseph, William and Thomas, bought much of the land. As the community grew with expansion around the ancient settlements of Cherry Tree and Machon Bank, the area became very desirable for the wealthy, for professional people and those in trade.

*OS map of 1905 showing the grounds of Shirley, Sharrow Bank and Clifford*

Some of the earliest and largest property is at the east end, as wealthier people gradually moved away from the smoky works in the valley. Sharrow Head House, now hidden behind properties around the roundabout, was owned by Rev Alexander MacKenzie (1754-1816), Vicar of St Paul's on Pinstone Street. Originally the home of John Battie, agent for the Marquis of Rockingham, Lord of the Manor of Ecclesall, it was rebuilt in 1763 to the designs of architect John Platt of Rotherham. In Sheffield Cathedral there is a marble memorial to MacKenzie by Francis Chantrey.

Shirley House (31 Psalter Lane) was built in 1885 (note the date stone and initials on the side of the house) by William Alexander Tyzack on a field called Southcroft. Tyzack owned Stella Works on Hereford Street, founded in 1868, making cast and spring steel, as well as saws and scythes. The

Shirley grounds comprised 5 acres with stables, carriage house, tennis lawn and fernery. It was bought in 1920 by the United Methodist Church for church meeting rooms; a church (now St Andrew's Psalter Lane), designed in traditional perpendicular style by JA Teather, was built in the grounds in 1930 when Marks & Spencer bought out the church on South Street, now The Moor.

Sharrow Mount House (30 Psalter Lane) opposite is a much altered Georgian house occupied in the 1880s by accountant Thomas George Shuttleworth, founder member and president of the Sheffield & District Society of Chartered Accountants. His offices were in the Queen's Insurance Building, Church Street. In the 1890s, the house was occupied by Captain Tolmie John Tresidder, director of John Brown steelworks, who in 1891 introduced a new technique for hardening compound armour plate under water sprinklers, producing a super hard surface.

A fine early brick house called Sharrow Bank (57 Psalter Lane) is no longer standing. It was bought in 1820 by Henry and Mary Newbould. Henry (1790-1871) was descended from Ecclesall yeomen. His grandfather Thomas (Master Cutler in 1751) leased Broomhall Wheel, and father Samuel (Master Cutler in 1800) moved the edge tool and saw-making business to Bridgefield Works in 1784. In a merger in 1900 they became Sanderson Brothers and Newbould. Henry's twin children John and Elizabeth lived in the house after his death. John (1822-1880) was an attorney with chambers at 4 Paradise Square. The house was sold by auction in March 1881, the sale lasting for 7 days, and was bought by Fanny and John Eaton, a pawnbroker and jeweller of 65-67 South Street. John was fifth Lord Mayor of Sheffield in 1900.

Between Wayland Road and Bagshot Street, a large house called Clifford was occupied in the early 1800s by snuff mill owner Thomas Wilson and managed by his widowed sister Mary Tenant. After Thomas died suddenly from a fall from his horse in 1819, Joseph Wilson (2) lived at Clifford till his death in 1829, then Joseph Wilson (3) owned the house but may never have lived there. By 1881 it was occupied by John Kitchin, owner of the Soho Cutlery Works at 13 Summerfield Street, manufacturers of table cutlery, knives and scissors.

The property came up for auction in 1887 - a *'substantially built family residence...together with extensive ornamental grounds, shrubberies, well-grown timber, ornamental lake, coach house, carriage house....The house contains tiled entrance hall, dining and drawing rooms, library, small cloak room, two kitchens, WC, 5 bedrooms, 2 attics....The outbuildings comprise 4 stall stable, carriage house, hay chamber, workroom, boot house, coal house, mushroom house, tool house......offers an excellent opportunity for the erection of two residences similar to Clifford....or a number of smaller villas....comprises 7 acres or thereabouts.'* Now terrace houses occupy the land.

**Albert Jahn**

Clifford School was built in 1832 on Joseph Wilson's land. It became a Church School attached to St Andrew's in 1869. It houses some William Morris stained glass and a memorial to Arnold Loosemore, the only Sheffield person to win a Victoria Cross in the First World War, removed from the demolished church on St Andrew's Road.

A workhouse Sharrow Mount (112 Psalter Lane), stood on land given by the Marquis of Rockingham in 1763, since the population had grown too large for the small workhouse on Cherry Tree Hill designed for 60-80 paupers. Following the 1834 Poor Law Amendment Act, Nether Edge Bierlow Union Workhouse was built in 1843, and Sharrow Mount was changed to private housing. Residents included Samuel Peace (1820-1889), a steel refiner on Well Meadow Street, and Albert and Francis Jahn. Albert was a craftsman in silver and enamel in Arts & Crafts style, and Principal of the Sheffield School of Art in 1905-1914; being of German origin, he was interned in 1914. Francis designed the Weston Park war memorial in 1923. All the houses of Sharrow Mount except one were demolished in the 1970s for new housing on Sandbeck Place; the drive still survives as a footpath.

Sharrow Cottage (110 Psalter Lane) is one of the earlier houses on the road – it was built in 1825 for the Vestry Clerk of Ecclesall Bierlow township. Minutes reveal the occupants. In 1830 James Richardson was dismissed for fraud, owing £328; he was succeeded by Benjamin Slater, who oversaw the 1831 census and was involved in the cholera outbreak in 1832 which led to an enquiry into the state of local water supplies. He died suddenly in 1844 aged 36, and had embezzled over £1,800.

On the junction of Psalter Lane and Kingfield Road once stood Psalter House (127 Psalter Lane), remodelled in 1866 to a Flockton design. It was lived in by William Sparrow, tailor and draper at 34 West Bar, who died in 1896, the same year as steel manufacturer Frederick Tyzack bought the house at auction. In 1936 Psalter House was occupied by solicitor Allan Hovey Styring, son of Alderman Robert Styring and Annie Frances Hovey, owners of Brinkcliffe Towers from 1902 up to Annie's death in 1925. Annie's father had a drapers and outfitters in Angel Street and Robert was Lord Mayor in 1906-07. Psalter House was demolished in the 1970s to make way for Kingfield Lodge and Synagogue.

Near the top of the hill was the Boys' Bluecoat School, built in 1911 by Gibbs and Flockton, on land owned and let for quarrying by the school since 1796. There is a plaque on the front of the building which records the school's history. A hundred orphaned boys were cared for with strict discipline; they wore a distinctive uniform of blue tailcoats with brass buttons, green corduroy trousers, white neckbands and blue muffin caps. By 1938 it was a College of Commerce with about a hundred students. The building was requisitioned in the Second World War as a transport depot; men were billeted in nearby houses and used the quarries as rifle ranges for target practice. After the War, it was an Emergency Teacher Training College, later housing the School of Art as part of Sheffield City Polytechnic. In the late 1950s, a range of 'contemporary' buildings with 'some classical character' were added, to be used for printing, decorating and silversmithing, and the old school building was the library. The buildings later became a campus of Sheffield Hallam University until its sale in 2008, for a housing development.

As the road increased in popularity, smaller houses started to be built – brick and stone detached properties such as West View (119 Psalter Lane), built in 1874 as the home of Henry Adams (1836-1906) whose father founded the Refuge Assurance Company in Pinstone Street. Henry built the row of houses opposite his own (128-136 Psalter Lane) as an investment for his daughter Gertrude. The family has a grand marble memorial just inside the gate of the General Cemetery on Cemetery Road. After the Second World War, the house became the Ministry of Pensions and National Insurance.

Further up the hill and shielded from view by trees are Storkholme (129 Psalter Lane) and Rockhills (131 Psalter Lane), imposing brick houses built around 1870. In 1910, Rockhills was the home of Jack Alexander, general manager of Hadfields Steel Foundry, and later became the base for St John's Ambulance.

A row of fine detached stone villas, built probably in the 1870s on the former Square and Turner Fields of John Hunter's farm, include Elmfield (192 Psalter Lane) which around 1912 was the home of Sheffield Microscopical Society, Portland House (190 Psalter Lane) which in 1910 became Burton's school, and 182 Psalter Lane which later became the Constance Grant School of Dance. 180 Psalter Lane was the home from about 1880 of Philip and John Unwin Askham, who founded steel casting manufacturers Askham Bros & Wilson Ltd in 1868 at the Yorkshire Steel works on Napier Street. The National Coal Board

*Frank Saltfleet*

occupied the house in the 1950s. Penrhyn Villa (174 Psalter Lane) is an interesting rendered house standing at right angles to its neighbours, of uncertain building date.

Rows of fine terraced houses built soon after 1900 infilled the spaces between these detached 19th century properties, occupied by a wide range of professional people. There were accountants and artists such as President of the Sheffield Society of Artists Frank Saltfleet (1860-1937) (11 Psalter Lane) known for his sea and landscapes. In 1904 he married Jean Mitchell, a landscape painter and daughter of Young Mitchell, for 20 years head of the School of Art on Arundel Street founded in 1843. Young believed, as did Ruskin, in the necessity of a partnership between the artist and the manufacturer, and in giving designers a sound artistic education.

At 132 Psalter Lane lived Albert Oswald Mosley (1880-1950), youngest son of Robert Fead Mosley, founder of the Portland Works on Randall Street, one of the earliest integrated metal workshops in Sheffield where stainless steel knives were first made. Albert ran the company after his father's death in 1926.

Builder Walter Shaw of 32 Psalter Lane was responsible for the fine semis with curved glass windows on the Clifford land. These were occupied by people such as Reverend William Odom (50 Psalter Lane), author of a number of books, printer Charles Bescoby (66 Psalter Lane), professional organist and composer Oswald Clayton Owrid (82 Psalter Lane) and English Steel Corporation manager Douglas Beardshaw (98 Psalter Lane).

Albert Harland (1869-1957), managing director of Wilson's Top Mill and grandson of Henry Wilson of Westbrook, lived at 10 Psalter Lane; the son of Rev Albert Augustus Harland from Middlesex, he married Louisa Wilson in 1865. He and William Thompson (who married Elizabeth Wilson) ran Westbrook Mill with Alfred Wilson. Other family members include Neville Harland (42 and 30 Psalter Lane) and John Wilson Harland (44 Psalter Lane), as well as Captain W Harland in Sharrow Green Cottage (4 Psalter Lane), built in 1795 by Reverend Alexander Mackenzie.

94 and 92 Psalter Lane were destroyed by a bomb during the December 1940 blitz and were completely rebuilt – notice their more modern style.

At the western end of the road, allotments occupying the fields on the north side were gradually built over. Some of them were occupied by quarry workers - Brincliffe Edge was a valuable sandstone quarry, exploited since the 15th century for cutlery grindstones and 'Brincliffe Blue' stone for windowsills and doorsteps, widely used in nearby houses. The painting by J. McIntyre of c1850 *'Sheffield from Psalter Lane'* in Museums Sheffield's collection records the evocative scene. There is a row of quarrymen's cottages on the edge; opposite them, cottages known as Salt Box Row were set against the rock face, were demolished in 1967.

————————

More detail about the properties along Psalter Lane can be found in the following paper, where the reader can follow the route as a round walk from Sharrow Head:

Morgan, R A, 'Psalter Lane in Sheffield - Walk along an Ancient Route', Transactions Hunter Archaeological Society 27 (2013) 45-83.

Flett, J, 'The Newboulds of Sharrow Bank', in They Lived in Sharrow and Nether Edge. (1988) 8-11.

Leng, W C Sheffield & District Who's Who (1905).

# PUBLIC TRANSPORT IN NETHER EDGE - from Bus Wars to Electric Trams.  John Baxendale

Nowadays you wouldn't see a horse in Nether Edge from one year to the next, but when our suburb was born horses were the only way of getting around - apart from walking.  The rich might keep a horse and carriage in the outbuildings that can still be seen behind the larger Victorian houses. For the moderately affluent there were cab stands at Byron Road and outside the Union Hotel, and horse-drawn buses like George Wright's, which

*Cab outside the Union Hotel*

in 1854 ran six times a day between Cherry Tree Hill and the new Market Hall in the town centre at a fare of 3d.   Wright's bus carried 31 passengers, twelve inside and nineteen on the top, and it required the upkeep of six horses to keep it running all day – a substantial enterprise.   The poor, as ever, would walk.

By the late 1860s George Wostenholm's land was rapidly being turned to housing, and the middle-class population of the area was rising. Wostenholm and Montgomery Roads had opened up, providing a more direct route to the city centre, and the newly formed Sheffield Carriage Company was running horse-drawn buses to Cherry Tree and Nether Edge seven times a day.  Advertisements for the new houses in Kenwood and Nether Edge invariably emphasised their proximity to the bus routes.

But seven buses a day were not enough for Thomas Steade, the pugnacious builder who developed much of the Wostenholm estate and owned many of the freeholds.  In 1869, encouraged by 'the certainty of good omnibus arrangements greatly increasing the value of property in the neighbourhood' he persuaded a group of local businessmen, including the cutlery manufacturer Henry Carr Booth, (who built Spring Leigh, the big house on Rundle Road) to set up the Brincliffe, Nether Edge and Sharrow Omnibus Company to run buses every half an hour.  The new company used stables at the top of Byron Road, and an adjoining coach-house on Edgebrook Road, which still stands.

A period of open warfare between the two companies ensued.  The competing buses were accused of 'furious driving', racing each other down the Moor at speeds of up to fifteen miles an hour. Steade was himself accused of evicting tenants who would not use his buses (which he denied), and repeatedly obstructing his rivals with his own carriage to slow them down and prevent them from picking up passengers. In a bizarre incident he was fined one shilling for allegedly striking a conductor with his umbrella while the two buses competed for the custom of two lady passengers on the Moor.

*Thomas Steade's bus*

But the writing was on the wall for the buses. In 1870 the Council was empowered to lay tramlines, and in December 1877 the (London-based) Sheffield Tramway Company started running horse-drawn trams every seven minutes from their newly built depot on Machon Bank Road (where Sainsbury's and the Nether Edge Garage now occupy some of the old sheds) following the same route along Moncrieff Road that the number 3 follows today, at a fare of 2d.

The original two bus companies withdrew from the fray, but Steade was made of sterner (or more reckless) stuff. He paid off the debts of his company in return for their horses and vehicles, reputedly taking a loss of some £4,000, and carried on running the buses himself in competition with the trams, employing familiar tactics. As a builder legitimately hauling bricks all over Nether Edge he could easily conjure up, as one resident put it, *'a Juggernaut looking cart with wheels of massive breadth...moving at a snail's pace in front of the tramcar',* and malicious intent was not easy to prove in court. After a year Steade was obliged to concede defeat, but his extravagant behaviour in the 'bus wars' presaged his spectacular bankruptcy a decade later.

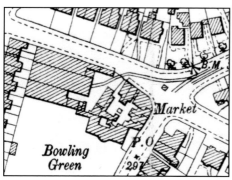

*1901 map showing tram lines, tram sheds and stables on Machon Bank*

Though still horse-drawn, trams were better than buses because (unless obstructed by Steade's wagons) they could move faster and more smoothly with fewer horses, and so running costs were lower and fares cheaper. But they were not without their problems.

In vain Kenwood residents petitioned the new company not to run trams on Sundays – not because Sunday was the Lord's Day, but because it was the working man's day off, and the trams might *'bring into the neighbourhood a class of people who do not come there at present...and will probably cause considerable damage to shrubs, trees, houses and gardens'* on which residents of these 'quiet and respectable' roads had spent much time and money. Did the 'Kenwoodites',

*Horse drawn tram at Nether Edge depot 1886*

then, retorted one critic, *'assume to possess more refinement than their fellow townsmen along other [tram] lines?'* And in any case *'hundreds of working men, with their wives and families'* habitually visited this still semi-rural spot of a Sunday, and why shouldn't they, since the roads leading to it were maintained and lighted at public expense?

*Tram and tip horse on Cemetery Rd*

More seriously, Sheffield's hills created problems for the trams, as they had for the buses, and an extra horse, called a 'tip-horse', was needed to haul them up Cemetery Road. Even on the flat and in the most expert hands horses were liable to bolt, and brakes were too primitive to hold them back: the papers were full of road accidents, often fatal. In 1899 a Nether Edge tramcar ran away down Cemetery Road, and three passengers who had unwisely jumped off were injured, one seriously.

A continuing problem was the private Tramway Company itself, accused of inadequately maintaining rolling stock, lines and roads, and being unresponsive to local needs. On the expiry of the lease in 1896 ownership of the tramway passed to the City Council, who proceeded to cut fares, improve working conditions, and electrify the system, starting with  the Tinsley to Nether Edge line in September 1899. Cheering crowds lined the streets not only for the ceremonial 'first tram' to Nether Edge, but for a trial run at midnight a few days earlier, and for days afterwards the Nether Edge trams were packed with day-trippers. The local newspapers were filled with lengthy descriptions of the inaugural run, and detailed articles about the technical aspects of the new system, its overhead cables, the generators at Kelham Island, and the trams themselves, some of which were built at the Nether Edge workshops.

This was modernity on wheels: vehicles propelled through the streets by the invisible power of a miraculous new technology in place of the sweat and

*Electric tram at Nether Edge*

toil of brute beasts. In the end, motor-cars and motor-buses would win out, driving the trams from the roads of Nether Edge in 1934, but in 1899 cars were still noisy, smelly  and unreliable, a rich man's toy , and accidents were frequent though rarely serious with a speed limit of 14 mph. (Leonard Slater, the owner of Spring Leigh, was fined £1 by Rotherham magistrates in 1908 for driving at 21 mph). But if fascination with modern technology drove popular enthusiasm for the trams so too did civic pride and the democratic spirit of that progressive age. Hero of the hour was a Liberal politician called Clegg – no, not that one, but William Clegg, the 'uncrowned king of Sheffield', and that year's Lord Mayor, who had guided the municipalisation of Sheffield's trams along with the electricity and water supply, in that age of 'gas and water socialism'. The words 'Sheffield Corporation Electric Tramways' on surviving rectangular manhole covers on Moncrieffe and Montgomery Roads and elsewhere stand as modest monuments to a moment of municipal enterprise and local pride in which Nether Edge played a brief but starring role.

# BRINCLIFFE BANK, UNION ROAD

## Susan Gudjohnsson

This is the story of Brincliffe Bank, one of the many beautiful houses with which Nether Edge is blessed. Or should that be two of the many beautiful houses? Today Brincliffe Bank stands as a pair of semi-detached houses at 94 and 96 Union Road, known as Glenholme and Beechwood repectively. The two houses have many lovely and interesting features

*Brincliffe Bank*

and both were served by a "never-failing spring" with a well and pump to each house. There were three substantial greenhouses at Glenholme and at one time there was a tennis court there, with ladies' pavillion sheltered on three sides by a magnificent yew hedge. Beneath the tennis court was an air raid shelter dating from the First World War.

The present owners were told that the original house was split into two dwellings somewhere around 1905, when the frontage to Glenholme was extended and enhanced with Art Nouveau features. I was intrigued and embarked upon some detective work.

Brincliffe Bank was built in 1857 by Richard Smith, a well-known portrait painter from an old Sheffield family. Mr. Smith seems to have had plenty of work with commissions from the great and the good of Sheffield. Among his many paintings is a portrait of Sir John Brown, founder of the Atlas Works in Brightside and Lord Mayor of Sheffield in 1861. In contrast, he also painted the poet John Holland, who was editor of the Sheffield Iris newspaper. There is no way of knowing how much of the design of the house came from the artist himself, but he left his mark with his initials on the gable of No. 94 and inside on the newel post there.

So in 1857 Brincliffe Bank became home to the Smith family household, which in addition to the artist, consisted of his wife Elizabeth, their 4 children and 2 servants, a total of 8 persons. This is actually rather a small household for a property that was later advertised as having a total of 8 bedrooms and 5 attics. It's perhaps not surprising therefore, to learn that within a very short space of time, Brincliffe Bank was home to a second family and it seems that within 3 years the house was already split into two semis. No. 94 was rented out to the Rev. Brooke Herford, who lived there with his wife, five children, a nurse, a cook and a domestic servant. Rev. Herford was pastor at the Unitarian Chapel on Norfolk Street for a number of years.

In 1868, the Herford's moved on and the Smith's moved down to 94. Number 96, now known as Beechwood, was leased to John Beatson, an iron merchant. Then, just three years later, in June 1871, the property was put up for auction as a pair of semi-detached dwellings. It is clear from the newspapers of the day that Richard Smith owned both houses and was selling them because he was in some financial difficulty. This begs the question 'was Brincliffe Bank ever a single property?' Or was it, as seems more likely, built as a pair of semis, with a view to achieving some rental income, perhaps to help out with the mortgage repayments?

*Richard Smith's initialled gable and newel post*

By 1873 the Smith's were living on Byron Road and the Herfords were gone, but the property remained in single ownership. It was bought by a widow, Mrs Jane Thorpe , who owned a confectioner's shop at 1 Fargate and who lived at Glenholme, while renting out Beechwood. After her death in 1902, Glenholme at least was bought by the Greensmith family, who made the changes to the house frontage, put in the existing driveway and enlarged the conservatory around 1906.

The houses have changed little since that time, but the story of their occupants continues.

# MOUNT PLEASANT
# Chris Venables

At the bottom of Sharrow Lane, sits Mount Pleasant, a large grade II listed red brick building that has dominated the area since 1786. It was built by John Platt on land Francis Hurt Sitwell had purchased in 1777. Born Francis Hurt, on marrying heiress Catherine Sitwell, he changed his surname to Sitwell  and inherited the Sitwell's Renishaw estate. The Sitwells were a wealthy family whose fortune had been made from coal mining and as ironmasters and landowners in Eckington for many centuries.  Francis Sitwell used Mount Pleasant (reported as having a total of 365 panes of glass in it) as his town house with his main residence at Renishaw Hall in Derbyshire. During his time at Mount Pleasant, the garden was not very extensive and Sharrow Lane was a dirt track through fields leading from London Road to Psalter Lane, with small farm huts as the only buildings along its entire length. Mount Pleasant was his winter residence until 1794 when he sold it to Samuel Broomhead Ward.

*Samuel Broomhead Ward*
*(1770-1849)*

Samuel, although only 24 years old, was a gentleman of private means, inherited from Joseph Ward, merchant, who had began his trade as a "hardware man" in Nether Edge and was to become Master Cutler in 1790. Samuel owned the Nether Edge Estate, which lay between Brincliffe Edge and Machon Bank and roughly between what is now Sandford Grove Road and Edgehill Road – in other words, what was Nether Edge Farm including the farmhouse (which later became the now demolished Brincliffe Oaks pub). In 1804 Samuel bought the two Chequer Fields and the Goose Green Field from Joseph Cecil and the allotments along the eastern boundary of Mount Pleasant. He made a walled park lined with trees which extended from the front gate in Sharrow Lane right round the corner and along London Road to the present Herschel Road.

In 1849 Mount Pleasant, now joined on Sharrow Lane by four more grand houses, was let, not sold, to Thomas Tillotson who lived there for 19 years. By the 1860s, due to overcrowding at the County of the West Riding of Yorkshire's county asylum in Wakefield, plans were made to build a second asylum near to Sheffield. Pending its development a temporary branch asylum was established at Mount Pleasant in 1868. Its staff of 9 looked after 6 male and 68 female resident patients for four years. In 1872 as the lease on the building was due to expire and Wadsley County Asylum (later to become Middlewood Hospital)

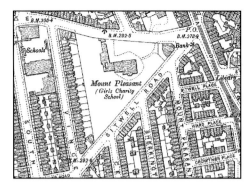

opened, the inmates at Mount Pleasant were all transferred to Wadsley.

Mount Pleasant then took on another identity as it was purchased in 1874 for the Girls' Charity School who relocated from St James' Row beside Sheffield Cathedral to the larger, more spacious surroundings of Sharrow. For 70 years the Girls' Charity School (renamed Mount Pleasant School for Girls in 1927) occupied Mount Pleasant and its grounds of three and a half acres, caring for 80 girls from 3 to 15 years of age - when they were considered old enough to work.  The girls were taught everything they would need for going into service and in doing so Mount Pleasant was kept in good working order.

*Old picture of Mount Pleasant*

Mount Pleasant was requisitioned for use by the Government during World War II and sited a Barrage Balloon in 1940. After the war, as well as still being a school, the building became a multi-use building used as bank clerk offices and by roofing contractors, the Coal Board, Refuge Assurance Company, Ministry of Engineering Works, the National Assistance Board (forerunner of the Department for Social Security) and as a driving test centre - remembered by many as "the Learners".

In 1903 the Sheffield School Board purchased some of the land bordering Sitwell Street to build a special school. The building opened in 1907 and catered for 80 children with learning disabilities on the ground floor and had rooms for teaching manual subjects and cookery on the upper floor. It was later used as a mainstream girls' high school until 1986 when it ceased to be a school. It is currently used as a youth centre known as 'The Hub'.

In August 1971 planning permission was rejected to pull down Mount Pleasant in order to extend Sharrow School; being Grade II* listed, saved Mount Pleasant and the Stables from demolition. After extensive renovation and alterations to the building, Mount Pleasant Community Centre opened to the public in April 1976, offering a large variety of courses and classes as well as housing a crèche and café, with a Youth Club in the Stables. In July 1988 the first Sharrow Festival was held in the house and grounds celebrating 200 years of Mount Pleasant. It was a lovely day and many hundreds of Sharrow residents enjoyed themselves. The building continued offering classes to the people of Sharrow until 2005 when Sheffield College, who had been based there since September 1994, pulled out.

*Mount Pleasant and the Stables today.*

Apart from occasional usage, Mount Pleasant stood empty until 2010 when, as caretaker students occupied it, the building began to show signs of life once again.

In January 2014, a property company called "Ad Hoc" leased Mount Pleasant from the council as "guardians" of the site. Local "social entrepreneurs" Pennie Raven and Jonny Douglas put forward proposals to turn the buildings and site into a cohousing, co-working "living lab" in the heart of Sharrow. Sheffield City Council rejected their plans and agreed in 2018 to sell Mount Pleasant to Hermes, a care firm. Following a £6.7 million transformation, they plan to convert it into a 30-bed care home. It is another building to watch with interest.

**Sources:**
http:/catherineclarke6.wixsite.com
In acknowledgement of the research conducted by Caroline Wells in 1995.

# SHARROW BANK, Family Home of the Newboulds, Tyzacks and Stephensons.
## Nick Waite

*Sharrow Bank in the 1930s*

Sharrow Bank is the only house in Nether Edge which was home to three notable local families. It was built in the early years of the 19th century, by father and son developers Dennis and Godfrey Sykes, on agricultural land acquired from the estate of William Fox. The substantial gentleman's residence on the corner of Cherry Tree Road and Psalter Lane had extensive grounds which extended as far as what is now Clifford Road.

It was purchased in 1820 by Henry Newbould and given the name of Sharrow Bank. Henry was the second generation of a successful manufacturing family, and the house remained a family home for the next 60 years. During that time Henry and his family embarked on a programme of land purchase in what would become the developing suburb of Nether Edge, as well as elsewhere in Sheffield.

The second notable occupants were one branch of the Tyzacks, whose occupation of a large number of houses in Nether Edge from 1885 onwards is told elsewhere in this book. William Tyzack was the great great grandson of the founder of W Tyack Sons and Turner. He bought the house in 1919 and it was home for his family until he sold it in 1936. Like the Newboulds, the Tyzacks were wealthy manufacturers, but their only contributions to Nether Edge's development were the houses where they lived. They came here because their fortunes were made initially in a string of water-powered sites in the valley of the Sheaf and subsequently, in the case of two branches of the family, in substantial factory premises to the North and South of the new Midland railway line.

Lastly came Colin Stephenson and his family; they had no fortune at all, but their careers exemplified the progress of social service from Victorian philanthropy to the Welfare State. They occupied the first floor of Sharrow Bank in increasingly straitened circumstances from 1936 to 1960.

## The Newboulds

Until his death in 1871 Henry Newbould purchased large plots of land between Sharrow Bank and what is now Osborne Road, as did his father-in-law William Williamson, whose land passed into the Newbould family through his daughter. Henry and Mary had four children, one of their sons died young and a second, William who was a clergyman, left Sheffield. The last of the family to live in Sharrow Bank were the unmarried twins John, a lawyer with offices in Paradise Square, and his sister Elizabeth.

When John died in 1880, the house and all its contents were sold by auction and in 1881 Elizabeth went to live near her cousin Samuel in Leamington Spa. In her accounts of the Newbould estate, Joan Flett describes in detail the seven day sale of the contents and the lifestyle it reveals; art works, an extensive library, household goods of great luxury, all within a large house and garden with three greenhouses and a staff of four servants. Subsequently there was a lengthy Chancery case about brother William's claim to one third of the estate. This was eventually settled by payments from Elizabeth in exchange for continued ownership of the family's Nether Edge lands.

Both Elizabeth and Samuel Newbould continued to purchase land towards the centre of Nether Edge, including the substantial eighteenth century house known as The Edge, which still stands on Ladysmith Avenue. In the large gardens of The Edge builder Henry Brumby constructed the present day Edgebrook Road, Ladysmith Avenue, Briar Road, Raven Road and Barkers Road. Brumby, like others building on Miss Newbould's land, had to comply strictly with the covenants she instructed her solicitors to impose.

 Similarly, before her death in 1909, she and her solicitors and surveyors had already laid out the Meadow Bank Avenue and Kingfield Estates on land in her ownership, with carefully drawn covenants as to construction and use of the properties which contributed materially to the quality of the housing and the social patterns of the area. There can be no question that the Newbould family's accumulation of land and careful control of its development were as significant as the Kenwood developments of George Wostenholm; they were both of crucial importance  in the creation of the Nether Edge we still enjoy today.

Following John Newbould's death and his sister's move to Leamington, the purchaser of Sharrow Bank was John Eaton, a pawnbroker with premises at 26-28 Corporation Street; he and his family lived there for nearly 30 years but at some time between 1907 and 1910 it was sold to Edward Holmes, a civil engineer and estate agent with offices at 16 St James Street,  During the Great War, Sharrow Bank was requisitioned by the War Office for temporary hospital use, and although the next owners had already agreed to purchase the property from the Holmes family, they were not able to complete the purchase and take possession until 1919.

## William Tyzack and family

After leaving home at 7 Williamson Road after his marriage, William Tyzack, (confusingly the fourth member of the family to share the name) lived at 9 Thornsett Road and remained there until he purchased the last and perhaps the grandest of the Tyzack mansions in Nether Edge, which the postal authorities had prosaically renamed 57 Psalter Lane but had been known as Sharrow Bank since 1820. This William was the fifth generation of the family to run (with his brother Samuel Meggitt Tyzack and his brother in law Colonel Middleton MC TD), what by then was the very substantial manufacturing company of W Tyzack Sons and Turner.

William's daughter Joan has left a sparkling memoir of the life she and her parents and brothers Brian and Peter enjoyed in what she described as a beautiful house with large grounds, indoor servants comprising a cook in button boots, a nursery maid and a parlour maid, with outside servants including a washer woman and a full time gardener to care for the extensive gardens, stables, garage and tennis court. Many parties were recollected, including a fancy dress party with one of her brothers and her seated on the grand piano, pretending to be toys.  To read Joan's account is to realise that what she remembered as a golden childhood describes how the most fortunate residents of our area lived in the 1920s and 1930s. Such times were never likely to be repeated. The wealth that made it possible derived from hard work and ambition in the mills and water-powered enterprises of the Sheaf valley.

Perhaps that golden life was not unclouded; the family only stayed in Sharrow Bank for 17 years. By 1936 the grandly named 'Sheffield Association for the Care of the Adult Deaf and Dumb' was searching for new premises. They wanted to leave the noise and dirt at the centre of an industrial city and relocate where their members could enjoy fresh air and grounds in which to play games and exercise. Why Sharrow Bank and its vibrant social life should be left by William and his family at that stage is unclear. His daughter Joan was only 16 or 17 and her recollections say nothing of the reasons; could it be that following some years of difficult trading conditions, the family income was no longer adequate to maintain the house and grounds and the expense of the lifestyle they enjoyed?  Or had they simply decided that Fulwood, on higher ground than Nether Edge and more socially exclusive, was preferable for them and their descendants?

## The Stephensons

When Sharrow Bank was sold in 1936 it needed renovation and adaptation to its new use; fortunately the price was only £2000, which even allowing for inflation in the intervening years seems extraordinarily low.  The Association was a charity established in 1862 by a group of philanthropists led by a Quaker steel manufacturing family, the Doncasters. The Sheffield Deaf and Dumb Institute they founded originally occupied premises in Division Street but by 1886 it was  providing substantial accommodation for the spiritual and temporal care of the profoundly deaf (and living quarters for the Superintendent and his family) in an ornate, Flemish-style building in Upper Charles Street.

From 1871 until his retirement at the age of 75 in 1920, the Superintendent, and only salaried employee, was George Stephenson. He was a Sheffield man who, until his appointment, had been a spring knife cutler like his deaf and dumb parents. It seems he got this job, as he was not deaf himself, by a combination of his knowledge of the disadvantaged community in which he was raised and the sign language which they used, with a sizeable chunk of chutzpah.  However he came to the job, he made it not only his own, but created a dynasty. Uniquely amongst the profession of Superintendent/ Missioners in the national chain of privately-funded, caring institutions for the deaf, four successive Stephensons were the guides (and sometimes authoritarian carers) for the Sheffield deaf community, until the Institute closed in 1960.

By 1936 the Association was in financial difficulties, with a static body of financial donors and increasing reliance on subventions from the Sheffield Corporation's Public Assistance Committee. Sharrow Bank was the perfect solution because, although considerable expenditure was needed for conversion, including a chapel, the Charles Street premises had been sold for £7000 and the Association had repaired the balance sheet, at least until the next crisis.

Of course the Association and the profoundly deaf members of the Institute did not "live in Nether Edge", but their Superintendents did. George

*Colin Stephenson in his lay preacher robes*

Stephenson was succeeded by his youngest son Colin in 1920, and after an uncomfortable few months camping on the floors of several accommodating church halls, he and his wife and three children moved to Sharrow Bank in 1936. Colin became well known in Nether Edge, a staunch supporter of St Andrew's and a diocesan lay reader, who preached to the deaf and dumb in sign language. The Stephensons were traditionally Wesleyans, but the Institute had been licensed for weddings by the Bishop in 1913, and older residents may remember Canon Reginald Robson of St Andrew's who was a member of the Institute's managing committee in its later years. The Institute and the Stephensons were remembered in her publications by our first local historian Mary Walton of Clifford Road. As City Librarian she recalled Colin serving with her on fire watching duties during the Blitz, stationed on the roof of the Central Library – quite a thought, as Colin had an artificial leg.

Colin Stephenson died in 1953 after 33 years of unremitting service in Charles Street and Sharrow Bank, and was succeeded by his 27 year old son Alan who, like his father, was born in the Institute and knew no other life. By then the Association was in difficulties, both political and financial. The City Council had decided to use the powers granted by Section 29 of the National Assistance Act of 1948, to set up its own deaf welfare service under the Public Health Committee. Efforts to negotiate an Agency Agreement with the Association had failed, largely because of irreconcilable differences of outlook between the Labour Council and the local businessmen who dominated the Association's Committee. From 1956 the Council withdrew the substantial grant which had bolstered the Institute's finances since Colin negotiated a deal in 1937. Alan Stephenson could see no future for himself as part of the Council's new department, and resigned in 1958. For the remaining two years the Association appointed his mother Doris, Colin's widow, as Superintendent, but this was only a stop gap and the Institute closed its doors in October 1960. The Council purchased Sharrow Bank and it was then used as a Handicapped Persons Centre until replaced by the modern premises on Grange Crescent in 1985. After that the house was empty until it was sold for development and then demolished around 1994.

The scheme approved by the Charity Commissioners to dispose of the

Institute's funds provided that Doris Stephenson was awarded a pension of "not more than" £2.50 per week for life, and she lived in rented flats in Travis Place, Cemetery Road and finally Wayland Road until her death in 1971. So ended almost a century of service to Sheffield's profoundly deaf by the Association and the Stephensons, and with it the 140 year history of Sharrow Bank as a family home.

## Resources:

*Whites and Kelly's Directories,* Sheffield Central Library, Local Studies.
'*They Lived in Sharrow and Nether Edge',* NENG 1988
'*Cherry Tree Hill and the Newbould Legacy'* Joan Flett NENG 1999
'*A History of the Parish of Sharrow Sheffield.'* Mary Walton 1968
'*Alone in a Silent World.'* Nick Waite Troubador Publishing 2016

---

# SHARROW HOUSE & ITS WELL

# Robert Grant

My one and only house move was when I married in 1964 and my wife and I bought a house in Huntingdon Crescent. Some of the other residents of the Crescent had lived there since the new houses were built in the late 1930s. The Crescent was in two parts, curving around from each end but not connected in the middle for road traffic, only a footpath as shown on this 1951 map.

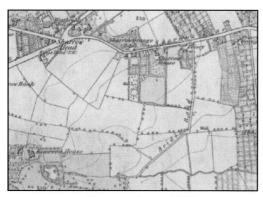

*Sharrow Lane 1851*

Some of the original residents mentioned that in this short piece of rough ground between the two parts of the Crescent there was a well. The Council made up the road between the two ends around 1970 but nothing was mentioned about a well. I was always intrigued by the layout of the Crescent with its ancient stone and brick boundary walls, a late 1930s development in an otherwise late Victorian area, so I started to do a little research and from old maps I found that there had been a dwelling called

Sharrow House where Huntingdon Crescent is now located.

In 1851 the houses starting from the bottom of Sharrow Lane on the left were Mount Pleasant then Priory Grange which would be near the junction of Wostenholm Road. Further up on the left was a building called Priory at the corner of a bridle road which became Priory Road then above this Sharrow House whose grounds extended from opposite where the bottom end of Grange Crescent is now up to the right hand bend at the top of Sharrow Lane.

There are also two buildings shown on the left side of this bend opposite Sharrow Grange which is on the right side of the road but I do not have any information about these. There was only one other house on the right side of Sharrow lane called Sharrow Head House in the 'V' between Sharrow Lane and Cemetery Road. Sharrow Head house is still there but is now accessed from Cemetery Road. The only other building close by was the Stags Head at Sharrow Head. Sharrow House had extensive grounds and beyond its own boundaries were open fields, looking across to the South West the next building was Kenwood House, now Kenwood Hall.

The first mention which I can find for Sharrow House is an advertisement for the sale of the house in The Sheffield Independent dated 29th May 1835 which reads *"For further particulars apply to the Owner and late Occupant, Mr. James Smith, The Priory, Sharrow Lane"*. Interestingly the ad mentions that there is an inexhaustible supply of soft water in the scullery and also a pump of pure spring water. More about this later at the end! Facilities also mentioned and detached from the House are enclosed Stable Yard,

TO BE SOLD BY PRIVATE CONTRACT,
**SHARROW HOUSE.**

AN excellent Modern Built comfortable HOUSE, calculated for the residence of a Family of the first respectability, situate in SHARROW LANE, surrounded by Pleasure Grounds, judiciously laid out, and commanding Views unrivalled for richness and variety; with a well-stocked Garden, Orchard filled with choice Fruit Trees in full bearing, and a Paddock of excellent Land, containing in the whole about Five Acres, all Freehold.

The HOUSE contains, on the Ground Floor, handsome Vestibule, capacious Dining and Drawing Rooms, of agreeable proportions, Kitchen, Scullery, Butler's Pantry, Store Room, &c. There are Six good Bed Rooms, and a cheerful Breakfast Room on the First Floor, with Dormitories in the Attics for Servants.

The Cellars are very good, and the offices replete with conveniences; an inexhaustible supply of Soft Water in the Scullery, and also a Pump of Pure Spring Water.

Detached from the House, is an enclosed Stable Yard, Stabling for Four Horses, Coach House with Mangle Room, and Hay Lofts over, Piggery, &c. &c.

The House is in Ornamental Repair, and ready for the immediate Occupancy of a Tenant, without further Outlay. For further particulars, apply to the owner and late Occupant, Mr JAMES SMITH, the Priory, Sharrow Lane. 29th May, 1835.

*Sale notice Sheffield Iris 1835*

Coach House with Mangle Room and Hay Loft over, Piggery, &c. &c.

In May 1836 at the Parish Church of Leeds Mr Joseph Levick of Endcliffe eldest son of Joseph Levick Esq. of Sharrow House near Sheffield married Susanna, only child of Ephraim Elsworth Esq. of Sandford House Kirkstall, so Joseph and Helen Levick must have been the purchasers. They are also listed in the 1841 Census along with 5 other people but as the 1841 Census does not list relationships or occupations we can only assume that they were probably servant, cook, coachman etc.

In the year of 1840 Mr Roger Gregory, an 'old and valued servant of Joseph Levick Esq., of Sharrow House, near this town', died and interestingly listed in the 1841 Census is Ann Gregory age 14. Was Ann already living there or was it a kindly act of Joseph to give Ann a home?

Helen Levick died in February 1845 at the age of 53 and 4 years later in 1849 Joseph put the house up for sale with this advertisement in the Sheffield Independent:

*'Sharrow House. Excellent Freehold Residence and Premises at Sharrow. To be sold by private contract or let for a term of years by Joseph Levick Esq., the owner. Messrs. W. and B. Wake, Solicitors, Sheffield, are authorised to handle the arrangements.'*

Once again turning to the Sheffield Independent we find the following entry for January 2nd 1850: 'Municipal Elections. William Fawcett, Sharrow House, Merchant'. William was of the same family as John Fawcett who had been a partner in William Greaves and sons in Sheaf Works.

After the Fawcetts moved out Thomas Jessop moved from Shirle House to Sharrow House sometime just before the 1861 Census, which gives his family details as Thomas Jessop, his wife Frances, two daughters and a son, and four servants. Thomas was born 31st January 1804, in the family home on Blast Lane situated next to the small steel works of his father William Jessop.

The British Association Handbook of 1910 gives the date of the founding of the firm William Jessop & Sons as 1774. The business prospered and eventually grew into a great international enterprise with the production of crucible steel for the cutlery trade, edge tools and engineering and with expanding markets in the United States moved to larger premises in Brightside. On the death of his father Thomas took over the business. As well as being a successful and wealthy business man Thomas had an active

public life in Sheffield. In 1843 he became a member of the Town Council, in 1863 Master Cutler and JP, and in 1863-64 Mayor. Thomas also founded the Jessop Hospital for Women which opened in 1878 at a cost of £26,000.

In 1869 his daughter Rebecca, married William Greaves Blake. Thomas Jessop and his wife went to live in Endcliffe Grange and William and Rebecca became the next occupants of Sharrow House. In 1873 Thomas Jessop made a settlement on his daughter, Rebecca Blake, and transferred ownership of Sharrow House to her.

The Blake family's typefounding business was started in the early 1800s and after various partnerships had been formed, dissolved and reformed became Stephenson Blake & Co. in 1839. Typefounders produced metal letters for type setters or compositors to rack up into blocks in a tray which was then used to produce a printed sheet. White's and Kelly's street directories for 1868-1883 list Stephenson Blake & Co. letter founders at 199 Upper Allen Street and 33 Aldersgate Street London E.C.

The Blake in this partnership was Thomas Blake and when he died in 1868 his interest in the firm passed to his son William Greaves Blake. For the whole of the rest of the nineteenth century and the first part of the twentieth century the business prospered. William Greaves Blake acquired other interests and led quite a busy life. In 1872 he joined the Ecclesall Board of Guardians and eventually became their chairman. He had a special interest in children's welfare and one ward of the Children's Hospital, Sheffield, was named after him. He was also a member of the School Board and was involved in the establishment of the Girls' High School in Sheffield. In 1871 he was made a West Riding Magistrate and three years later he joined the Sheffield Bench. In 1877 he became a Guardian of the Assay Office joining his father-in-law Thomas Jessop.

A book with the title *'A South Yorkshire Family of Type Founders'* by William Greaves Blake, grandson of the typefounder, has a photograph of Sharrow House dated 1870 showing Major and Mrs W G Blake (and staff), Miss Eliza Jessop and baby Frances Blake.

In June 1881 William Greaves Blake bought at auction part of the Ecclesall Grange Estate consisting of land in Button Hill and Millhouses Lane. William built a new stone mansion neo gothic in style and with a castellated tower. The house was large and cost £14,000, an enormous sum in those days, William needed the extra space to house his growing family. The name given to the mansion house was Mylnhurst. William moved to Mylnhurst in 1883 and lived there until his death in 1904 but his widow continued living at Mylnhurst until her death in 1920 when the house was sold to W. J. Walsh owner of the department store on High Street, Sheffield.

The next occupants of Sharrow House when the Greaves Blakes moved out in 1883 were Leonard Edward Colley and Jonathan Colley, Tanners and leather merchants.

1901 saw the next owners move in. Jonathan Longbotham in the 1901 Census was aged 50, M.Inst. C.E. Mining & Civil Engineer with premises at 6, 7 & 8 Foster's Buildings, High Street. Hugh Ashley Longbotham, his son age 20, was a coal merchant's assistant, and George Norman Longbotham, his son age 19, was a mining engineering pupil. White's directory for 1903 lists H. A. Longbotham as coal & coke merchants with extensive depots at Harvest Lane, Rowland Street, Park Station, Pond Street Station, Brightside Wharf, Upwell Street, Wadsley Bridge and Midland Coal Depot, Chesterfield Road. They did not stay long and an auction notice appeared in the Sheffield Daily Telegraph of April 4th 1905:

*Now on view at THE MART, High Street, Sheffield. Household Furniture by Wm. Johnson & Sons, T. B. W. Cockayne and other noted local Cabinet*

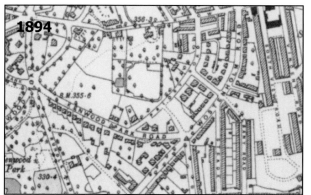

*Makers. Surplus from Jonathan Longbotham esq., Sharrow House, who is changing his residence.*

On Friday the 24th November 1911 the Sheffield Daily Telegraph reported the death of Jonathan Longbotham in a piece which runs to probably six column inches:

*'A prominent figure in the mining world he died at his London address in Northwood. He had an office in London but maintained close business relationships with Sheffield and South Yorkshire collieries. He was a consulting engineer for the North Eastern Railway. He came to Sheffield about 10 years ago from Durham and resided at Sharrow House but due to the unsatisfactory state of health of members of his family he was obliged to leave Sheffield and moved to Northwood, London. During the last five years Mr. Longbotham's health had been far from satisfactory and about six months ago his condition gave considerable anxiety to his family but he rallied. His health, however, remained very precarious. He was comparatively well on Saturday last but on Sunday internal haemorrhage began and he gradually sank and passed away yesterday.'*

Jonathan's will proved at £39,552 published 20th February 1912 would be equivalent to about £4½ million today.

The next reference which I can find for Sharrow House is in White's directory for 1910 and lists Herbert Edward Sandford, Solicitor and Commissioner for Oaths of 16 St. James Row as the occupant. In the Sheffield Evening Telegraph 26th Nov. 1910 Mrs. Herbert Sandford (Sharrow House) is recorded as donating £1 towards the K. H. B. Christmas Party to give a treat to 5000 of the poorest children in Sheffield at The Artillery Drill Hall.

The children will be brought in special tramcars to the Hall, fed and entertained for two hours and a half and then they return by tram to their respective districts, all in charge of the kind hearted teachers to whom so much of the success of the organisation has been due in the past.

The next residents of Sharrow House were John George Chapman and his wife. The company of Fletcher, Chapman and Cawood was registered on 12th January 1911 to deal in coal, coke, iron, steel, timber, granite and other materials. On the 20th April 1912 Harry Taylor, gardener, (40) was sent to prison with hard labour for six weeks for stealing from his employer, Mr. John George Chapman, coal and iron merchant, of Sharrow House, Sheffield, a quantity of garden implements, tools and motor clothing of the total value of £10. Mrs. Chapman in giving evidence pleaded for lenient treatment.

The Chapmans were involved in public life and on the 12th July 1912 it is reported that an Indian Prince visited Sheffield and that the arrangements for his tour were made by Mrs. Chapman of Sharrow House. His Highness the Maharaj Rana of Dholpar Rajputana earlier in the week visited Tinsley Park Colliery and went down the pit and also visited various engineering companies. In the afternoon they motored into Derbyshire and visited Haddon Hall and Chatsworth. In the evening the Prince dined at Sharrow House. Whilst in Sheffield the Prince stayed at the Grand Hotel.

On Saturday July 13th 1912 a sale of work was held in the grounds of Sharrow House in aid of the two Sharrow cots in the Bradstock Lockett Home for Crippled Children, Southport. The Northern Children's Union which was associated with the Church of England Waifs and Strays Society acknowledges the gardens being kindly lent by Mr. & Mrs. Chapman. If wet the event was to take place in the Clifford Schools. The weather was evidently favourable because a report on the 15th July says that it was a delightful fete and sale of work in the gardens of Sharrow House but does not mention how much was raised.

The Chapmans stayed until 1916 when George Allen Wilson moved in with his family and in May 1916 Mrs. Wilson was advertising for a nurse for 2 children. In 1919 there was an advertisement for the sale of a nanny goat and kid. Also in 1919 Mrs. Wilson was advertising for a gardener and then in July 1921 a garden fete was held to raise money for a Babies' Home. 1922 Mrs. Wilson advertised for a cook. The 1922 White's Directory is the first instance I have found of Sharrow House being given a house number: 223 Sharrow Lane, George Allen Wilson B.A. Solicitor.

The house itself had remained the property of Jonathan Longbotham when he moved to London in 1905 and of his heirs after he died in 1912, and was rented out to subsequent occupants. However, on 20th October 1923 an advertisement appeared for the sale of Sharrow House on Tuesday November 20th

*Re Jonathan Longbotham, Esq., deceased.*

*SHARROW HOUSE ESTATE, A VALUABLE BUILDING SITE WITH NEARLY 700 FEET FRONTAGE TO SHARROW LANE AND 135 FEET TO THORNSETT ROAD.*

The reference to 135 feet frontage to Thornsett Road is of interest as Thornsett Road was newly built, partly on land formerly belonging to

Sharrow House, as we can see from the two maps. I could not find any details for the sale of the land on the southern edge of the estate so we do not know if the Longbothams or a previous owner sold it.

The comprehensive sale notice for Sharrow House stated that the estate comprised Sharrow Lodge with vacant possession, formerly occupied by Alderman J. R. Wheatley, deceased, and Sharrow House, in the occupation of George A. Wilson Esq. A further advertisement appeared on November 3rd 1923 stating an upset price of £5000 and another update on November 17th informed potential buyers that the tenancy of George A. Wilson would expire on 25th March next. The auction took place on November 21st 1923 at the Sheffield Auction Mart, 2 High Street under the auspices of Messrs Nicholson, Barber and Hastings. However, the property was withdrawn as bids had failed to meet the upset price of £5000. It was offered for sale by private treaty, and on March 6th 1924, furniture removed from Sharrow House was offered for sale by J. J. Greaves and Sons.

However, a buyer did eventually appear, as explained in the following article from the Sheffield Daily Telegraph of 21st January 1925:

*'Since the scheme of training unemployed girls in domestic work was started, the classes have been carried out in different schools. During the autumn [of 1924], however, the opportunity of obtaining a house in which all the classes could meet, and in which a real training in housewifery was gained in a house, not a school, was considered advisable.'*

Sharrow House was considered a suitable centre as 'it is a well built residence and near the trams'. As the house had been standing empty for a few months much cleaning had to be done. This was undertaken by the girls, who also, under supervision, repainted several of the floors and distempered the staff sitting room.

1935

In November 1926 The Sheffield Daily Independent reported that the Training Centre was about to provide its sixteenth course for unemployed girls;

*'The training lasts for 13 weeks and each intake accommodates 72 trainees. During this time the girls are initiated into the skilled work, for domestic work is of a skilled character, of*

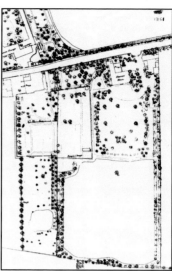

all that appertains to the domestic arts. The present intake of girls are nearing the end of their training and the principal of the Centre will interview ladies requiring maids on Monday, Tuesday and Wednesday of next week and the same days of the week following, the girls will of course be there.'

On the 11th November 1927 a 'Parents' Day' was held.

*'The smart and pleasant appearance of the girls at the Sheffield Centre is always commented on by members of the Central Committee for Women's Training and Employment (who are responsible for these classes) and yesterday the girls, each wearing her uniform made by herself, welcomed their parents and upheld well the reputation of the centre.'*

The Sheffield Daily Independent reported on Saturday 22nd March 1930 that since June 1921 approximately 2000 women had passed through the successive courses, which were run four times a year, first at various schools and then at Sharrow House. However, the notorious 'servant problem' was looming. Towards the end of 1930 The Independent ran an article entitled 'Why Servants Are Hard To Get'. 'Nights Off' appeared to be the main objection to taking up domestic service.

*'There are scores of openings waiting for girls in domestic service but very few girls willing to take them mainly because they cannot have nights off like typists and shop assistants. Even when girls have been through the excellent servants' training at Sharrow House which is run by the Employment Exchange and a good deal of Government money has been spent on them they sometimes decide at the last moment that they will not have housework.'*

Could this be that times were changing and was this the writing on the wall for Sharrow House? The Independent on Saturday 28th April 1934 reported that women and girls were enjoying a boom period in employment. Mirror polishers in the cutlery trade were 'almost at a premium', with the consequence that domestic service was becoming more unpopular. Only 19 girls had applied for training at the Sharrow House centre that term. The article compares wages for girls in the cutlery trade from 12s 6d to 25 shillings per week depending on service and experience as against domestic service weekly wage of 10s with full board. It also mentions that the Sharrow House course had been cut from 13 to 8 weeks.

The Sheffield Independent Saturday 30th March 1935 reported that;

*'Sheffield's domestic training centre for unemployed women and girls has been moved from Sharrow House, which is to be demolished for building purposes, to 76 Clarkehouse Road. This new house is a great improvement upon the old rambling house in Sharrow Lane. Electric light and electric cookers are installed and the training will be more in keeping with labour saving methods of modern houses.'*

Sharrow House was subsequently demolished.

## The Wells of Sharrow House

Numerous pumps and troughs are shown on the large-scale 1851 map, and on the lower side of the Crescent there is always water running on top of the underground clay on which the houses are built.

In 2004/5 a depression appeared in the middle of the road, nothing dangerous, just a 4 foot diameter circle about 2 inches deep in the centre, 53 feet from Sharrow Lane on the lower part of the Crescent. The Council came round and filled this depression with Tarmac. After a few months this happened again and then again. 2007 was a particularly wet year and in the autumn the depth of the depression was about 4 inches, always full of rainwater. When the Council came round again they marked out a square in yellow paint around the depression with the words 'TRIAL HOLE', something was obviously happening underground. Fortunately I came home while the workmen were there on 6th December 2007 and they had dug a couple of feet deep and were filling in with concrete. What they had found was the top of a circular brick shaft - see photo below left. Following measurements taken from Sharrow Lane and the kerb line on Huntingdon Crescent this would appear to be the well for the pump shown in the yard of Sharrow House on the 1851 map. I took a photo of the Tarmac patch which covered the concrete, before Huntingdon Crescent was resurfaced in 2017. See below right.

# SHIRLEY & ST.ANDREW'S PSALTER LANE
## Shelagh Woolliscroft

*Shirley*

The story begins in 1881 when William Alexander Tyzack purchased five acres of land from Elizabeth Newbould and her brother, who lived at Sharrow Bank. The Newbould family had acquired extensive land holdings in the area, as recorded elsewhere in this book and in NENG publications 'Cherry Tree Hill and the Newbould Legacy' and 'They lived in Sharrow and Nether Edge'. This piece of land was almost certainly part of Cherry Tree Farm which had been bought by Elizabeth's father, Henry Newbould, in 1840.The plot was bordered by Psalter Lane to the north and Cherry Tree Road to the west. George Wostenholm of Kenwood Hall had acquired much of the area to the south and east for his Kenwood estate: several large properties were already established on Kenwood Bank and Kenwood Road. The original conveyance has not been traced although one resident of Cherry Tree Drive has a document which includes a reference to covenants and indentures made between 1871 and 1881. The parties included William Alexander Tyzack,

*Shirley date stone*

Elizabeth Newbould and Reverend William Williamson Newbould. No further details exist but it is generally known that Elizabeth Newbould was careful to sell land subject to requirements which would retain the attractiveness of the area: it may be that she did so in this case.

*Shirley Agriculture and Commerce window*

William Alexander Tyzack was born in about 1836 in Ecclesall. He was a grandson of William Tyzack the scythemaker, who founded W Tyzack and Sons, with premises in Rockingham Street, Trafalgar Street and, memorably, Abbeydale Works (now Abbeydale Industrial

*Sale Plan of Shirley*

Hamlet). A more detailed history of the Tyzack family and their connections with Nether Edge can be found in Nick Waite's article. When William died his three sons carried on the business, expanding to new premises on Little London Road, but when the eldest son, Ebenezer, died in 1867 the other sons and nephews decided to set up what became rival businesses, all making scythes, sickles and other edge tools. William Alexander, the son of Ebenezer, acquired premises on Hereford Street, just north of St Mary's roundabout and set up W A Tyzack Ltd, initially employing 20 men. Most of their products were sold under the 'Horseman' brand. William was reputedly a very good salesman, travelling abroad extensively including to Russia, and the business prospered.

At that time William Alexander was living at 119 Priory Villas, Wostenholme Road, with his wife Elizabeth, son Ebenezer, a daughter Elizabeth (who died young) and three servants. By 1881 he had moved with his wife and three sons to Oak Lodge on Kenwood Bank and was purchasing the land for a new house, grand enough to reflect his growing status. By 1885 the house, number 31 Psalter Lane and later known as 'Shirley', was completed - see datestone and initials WAT on the side of Shirley House – on the field "Shire Ley" bought by his father, Ebenezer Tyzack, in 1851.

We learn from the later sale particulars that the house 'was built regardless of cost in a most substantial manner.' Access was from the corner of Psalter Lane and Cherry Tree Road via an imposing carriage drive through landscaped gardens. Although the grounds are much altered the house has stood the test of time and today it is much as it was in its heyday. The ground floor rooms included a billiard room 27x18 feet, a dining room 26 x18 (these two have been knocked together to provide a large meeting room), drawing room, morning room and smoke room. The ground floor had a central

*Shirley House 2013*

heating system. A large imposing hallway led to a staircase with a huge stained glass window depicting War, Peace, Agriculture and Commerce.

There were eight bedrooms, two with 'lavatory basins', and a separate bathroom and WC. The servants' department included two maids' bedrooms, three box-rooms, linen room, laundry room, pantry and cistern room. The main entrance faced west and adjacent to the southern side were various outbuildings including a coal store and laundry room, stables, loose boxes, harness room, carriage house and, by 1912, a motor shed. In the extensive grounds were a tennis lawn (two courts), a kitchen garden, greenhouse, a large heated frame and a fernery. In the remaining gardens were two summer houses and a large paddock.

William Alexander was at the height of his career when he died suddenly in December 1889, aged about 63.   At probate his estate was valued at over £52,000.  His widow Elizabeth inherited for her lifetime and remained there with their three sons, William, Ebenezer and John Stanley.   William and Ebenezer moved out when they married and in the 1901 census records there is only John Stanley, aged 23, living there with his mother and four servants.  Elizabeth died in 1912 and a new chapter began in the history of the house.

Shirley was put up for auction in 1912 but it appears that the estate was not sold.  The lack of an entry in any directory between 1912 and 1925 suggests that it was uninhabited. The entire estate was finally sold in 1923 for £4,550 to the members of South Street New Connexion Methodist Chapel who wished to relocate their place of worship in South Street (now the Moor) to a more populous area.  William Tyzack signed the conveyance as executor of his father's will.

For several years Shirley was used for Sunday school, recreation and for church services and between 1925 and 1968 the house was used for a Montessori kindergarten. There was a resident caretaker.  In 1930 the new church was completed, built of 'Stone Edge' stone obtained from the Stoke Hall quarry at Grindleford.

Shirley's tennis courts and paddock remained and were occasionally used for garden parties.  An area of the former gardens between the house and the church was at some point earmarked for a church hall. This was not pursued and the plot, together with the adjacent tennis courts, was sold to the Methodist Homes for the Aged who built the Southcroft apartments for elderly people on it.   Another plot to the west of the church and fronting

Cherry Tree Road was proposed for a manse but the building was never erected and the land now forms a memorial garden and ecological site.

Shirley House, as it has come to be known, is currently let out to a variety of organisations on a room by room basis in addition to being the church office. In 2012, following local fundraising, the house was updated to include disabled access and an interfaith room was created.

In 1964 the Methodist Church sold about two acres of land, comprising the former paddock and kitchen gardens, to Eric Taylor, of Newhome Properties, Dore. The sale price was £17,000 and the conveyance allowed for the construction of up to 16 one or two-storey detached houses (this was later varied to 19). The Methodist Church followed the example of Elizabeth Newbould in writing certain requirements into the conveyance. The properties were to be built of reconstructed stone or stone-coloured bricks; and for the roofs there was a choice of Hardrow stone slates, Westmorland slates or Cotswold grey tiles. Hardwood timber fences were to divide the plots and two-foot high natural stone walls with planting troughs were required at the pavement edge of each property. The only trade or profession permitted to be carried out from the houses was that of medical practitioner.

Newhome Properties were required to build a new access drive to the boiler house at the rear of the church, re-using the stone gateposts and iron gates from the former access drive in what is now the garden of Number One, Cherry Tree Drive. According to one of the bricklayers, Roy Mitchell, Eric Taylor built houses all over Sheffield and also worked as a surveyor for Hassall Homes. He lived at Ashfurlong Road, Dore. He was a perfectionist who believed in a job being done well and he inspected the work regularly. He used the best craftsmen (who all worked on a self-employed basis), paid good wages and treated people fairly: as a result people who worked for him tended to stay with him. Roy recalls that Eric Taylor used a Belgian architect who adapted his basic design to ensure that all the properties would be different. Some were two-storey, most were bungalows. All were fronted in an Anstone stone composite made by Forticrete of Kiveton Park - the same quarry that had supplied the stone for the Houses of Parliament. The architect put his personal stamp on them - he hand-painted a galleon on each chimney breast! Ducted air heating was installed in all 19 properties and has been retained in a few, though the majority of owners have since switched to radiator systems. Each house had a gleaming Hygena kitchen. The one in Number 17 lasted over fifty years!

*St. Andrew's Psalter Lane*

The conveyance stipulated that the houses were to be sold for a minimum of £4,500. In fact they were sold for £8,000 - £11,000, according to size and position. This was quite a high price in those days but people were happy to pay for good quality houses. Newhome Properties sold the freehold to a London company and most owners took up a subsequent opportunity to purchase the freehold.

The nineteen properties on Cherry Tree Drive were built over the two-year year period 1964-1966. In its early history the road could boast of two of Sheffield City Council's Chief Officers as residents – The City Treasurer, F.G. Jones, lived at number 4 and the City's Director of Education, T. Harold Tunn, lived at number 19. Some properties have been extended or adapted over the ensuing 50 years but without detriment to the overall character. Most of the original boundary walls remain and the road has retained an attractive and unified appearance.

In 1998 due to a declining congregation, Psalter Lane Methodist Church amalgamated with the Parish Church of St Andrew's, Sharrow, on St Andrew's Road, which, having been declared structurally unsound was demolished. The ecumenical church was renamed and following refurbishment of the church the stunning 'New Creation Window' was created by Rona Moody in 2002, to fill the interior with glowing light. The clock and bells of the old parish church are currently housed in a private museum in Dorset together with a brass plaque which reads:

'TO THE GLORY OF GOD.  THE CLOCK AND BELLS WERE PLACED IN THIS TOWER AS A LASTING MEMORIAL TO WILLIAM ALEXANDER TYZACK.

BY HIS WIFE AND THREE SONS.  AUGUST 1892'

**Sources:**
*Cherry Tree Hill and the Newbould Legacy.* Joan Flett
*A History of the Parish of Sharrow.*  Mary Walton
'*A Brief Guide to St Andrew's Psalter Lane Church*'
*Shirley, The Story of the House.* Joan Flett
'*Glass, Tools and Tyzacks.*' Don Tyzack
In acknowledgement of the research conducted by  Cherry Tree Drive residents - Roger Eyre, Kevin Garner and John Jenkinson.

# TWO CRESCENT ROAD VIGNETTES

## John Haigh

Crescent Road is a run of small villas erected by the famous builder Thomas Steade in the 1860s. Although much of a piece, they are all very different in detailed design. Many of them include decorative ironwork around the windows – a business sideline of Mr Steade's. The early occupants were small businessmen, 'little mesters'

*65 Crescent Road*

and skilled technical employees at the companies in the city. Here are two notes about early inhabitants that I have uncovered in my researches.

The first concerns number 65. In the 1870s a newly married couple James and Mary Huxley came to live there. He worked as a metallurgist in a local steelworks. (Later they moved to Kenwood Park Road). James was the nephew of an illustrious man, my personal great hero, Thomas Henry Huxley, the man most responsible for the rise in prominence and prestige of scientific thinking in influential circles post 1860, and famous for fiercely defending and establishing the ideas of Darwin - 'Darwin's bulldog' as he was known. At one time he was President of the Royal Society, Britain's highest scientific honour.

In 1879, the annual meeting of the British Association for the Advancement of Science was held at the University in Sheffield, and Huxley, who was a Vice Chairman, stayed with his nephew for the duration of the meeting. In his fifties and at the peak of his celebrity, he did not present a lecture at the meeting, but I imagine him being lionised and sitting back to listen to the contributions, including a sermon by the Archbishop of York

*Thomas Henry Huxley*

(incredible nowadays to think of a keynote sermon at a scientific meeting). Since his nephew was a technical man, I imagine the breakfast conversations at number 65 for those few days would have been well worth overhearing. The early days of controversy caused by the publication of Origin of Species were twenty years in the past and the Anglican Church, very wisely, was not actively opposing Darwin's and Huxley's ideas, but the Archbishop in his sermon put up a staunch defence of traditional Church teaching. Huxley himself was an agnostic, as was Darwin, largely I think because they did not feel they could oppose the elderly but still fierce lion of religion with the lively and growing fox terrier of science.

The second note concerns contemporary events at number 57, a few doors down from 65. Barbara Broomhead was the young unmarried daughter of an influential lawyer in Paradise Square. At the time of the building of Crescent Road she appears to have inherited money from her grandmother, and wisely and unusually she invested it in buying 57 as its first owner. Possibly this would have caused a stir in the locality. But the inevitable happened in that she fell victim to a gold-digging man called

*57 Crescent Road*

Robert Rowland St Leger Morrison. He was an architect, the son of a clergyman in Halifax, originally from Ireland.

Robert and Barbara then were married. From inference I think she must have been sensible enough to retain ownership of her house. It was probably useful to have a father as source of legal advice. She became pregnant and her husband lost his ardour, becoming the familiar type of patriarchal bully. She was reported at his trial as being a mass of bruises. The worst moment for her was his bringing into the house a frog from the garden to terrify her. She either took him to court for assault or saw to it that he was prosecuted and he was given the option of a fine or imprisonment. Having no money of his own he opted for the latter, moved out and disappeared from the record except that I found an itinerant man arrested many years later under his name. Barbara Morrison lived on at 57 until the turn of the century, with her daughter, giving her occupation on censuses as 'wife of an architect'. Several of the features of the house when we took over in 1997 appear to date from Barbara's time. A remarkable woman.

# ELECTRIC LIGHT AT THE BRINCLIFFE OAKS
## John Baxendale

One snowy night in November 1878, patrons of the Brincliffe Oaks Hotel and Bowling Green on Oakhill Road were granted a glimpse of the future. John Tasker, Sheffield's great electrical pioneer, the man who had already set up the first telephone exchange outside London, was demonstrating the electric light. As the Sheffield Independent's reporter rhapsodised, '*Snow had just fallen, and the green, arbour, and surrounding foliage were clothed in light. The electric light, thrown from a window in the second storey of the hotel, illumined the grounds with a dazzling radiance, heightened as it fell upon the glistening snow, and strangely contrasting with the dark shadows which, at the present stage of the invention, seem inseparable from the irradiation of the light,*' before going on to explain the technicalities in all the detail practical Sheffielders could wish for. As all loyal Blades know, barely a month earlier the world's first floodlit football match, also illuminated by Tasker, had taken place at Bramall Lane. It had been hoped to stage floodlit bowls at the Brincliffe Oaks, but the snow prevented it; however the scene was all the more picturesque, and the attending crowd pronounced themselves well satisfied.

1878 was in some ways the annus mirabilis of electricity. Niggling technical problems had been solved, and it was now feasible to supply electric power to a whole city. Nevertheless, it was not until around the turn of the century that electric supply became commonplace in the larger houses of Nether Edge. Until the infrastructure of generators and cables had been established and customers won over, electricity was a much more expensive way of lighting your house than gas, although brighter, cleaner and

altogether more pleasant to live with. The gadgets and appliances which make electricity indispensable today were still in the future. Although factories and large shops were connected on a one-off basis, it was not until 1892 that Tasker's Sheffield Electric Light and Power

Company was licensed to lay cables throughout the city – and then, as with cable TV, it was a matter of whether householders chose to take the plunge and get connected. In 1898 the company, as a natural monopoly, was taken over by the Council in the heyday of municipal enterprise led by the Lord Mayor, William Clegg, who as a young man had been one of the opposing captains in the floodlit football match of 1878.

The rate and pattern of electricity's spread through Nether Edge is not easy to trace, but you may find evidence under your feet. If you see a manhole cover marked 'Sheffield Electric Light and Power Company', that means the cable beneath was first laid between 1892 and 1899, in the days before municipalisation. So, eyes to the ground, but don't bump into any trees.

---

# NETHER EDGE'S SEWER GAS LAMP

## Chris Venables

These lamps, properly called Webb's Sewer Gas Extractor and Destructor lamps, with heavy cast-iron columns and fine circular lanterns, were invented by Joseph E Webb of Birmingham in the late 19th century and first patented in 1895. They were designed to perform the useful action of extracting and converting sewer gas to a harmless state by heat, at the rate of 11,500 cubic feet an hour. When applying for a patent, Joseph Edmund Webb summarized his Sewer Gas Destructor and Destructor lamp as follows:

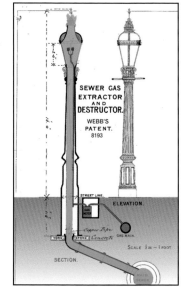

*The object of the invention is to extract the obnoxious gases and vapour collected or generated from a sewer and at the same time to effectually destroy all germs and noxious qualities prior to their passing into the atmosphere. For this purpose I propose to utilise ordinary lighting gas which may at the same time be used for street or other lighting purposes.*

Sewer gas was extracted by convection from the main sewerage system. It was drawn up a

*Webb's patent drawing showing the separate town gas supply to the burners*

large diameter tube (hence the bigger diameter of the column compared to ordinary gas lamps) to the head of the lamp by means of gas burners (with three no. 2 mantles) which were operated by town gas. The temperature, between 600 - 700 degrees Fahrenheit, was sufficient to destroy smells and bacteria as the gas from the sewer passed through the lamp to the open air. The rate of extraction was claimed to be capable of ventilating a ¼ mile of sewer.

Eighty-four Webb Lamps were erected in Sheffield between 1914 and 1935, the largest number in any British town, and due mainly to Sheffield's many hills where gas pockets might accumulate. The Brincliffe Edge Road / Union Road lamp was the first to be erected in 1914, followed by the Cemetery Road / Frog Walk one in June 1915. Three other local lamps, which ceased to exist many years ago, were:

Lamp no. 6: erected 1915 at Machon Bank Rd/ Union Rd.

Lamp no. 20: erected 1916 at Kingfield Rd/ St Andrew's Rd

Lamp no. 22: erected 1917 beside St Andrew's Church, St Andrew's Rd.

Advertising by the company pointed out that independent tests had showed that the sewer gas destructor lamps used no more gas than ordinary lamps but that the illumination was increased by at least 5% with 'newspaper type being read at 50 yards', so you received three benefits (ventilation, sterilisation and more light) for no extra running cost as well as clothing aesthetically something which had an unaesthetic purpose.

The need for the sewer lamp ventilation system declined following changes in the design of sewerage and drainage systems including laying house connections from private drains to the sewers enabling the sewer to be ventilated through the vent pipe of the house drain and the use of stack pipes running up to roof level at the head of the house drains. The County Engineer's Department removed them as the opportunity arose and by 1978 only 36 remained. Following protests, press and TV publicity, further removal was deferred pending review.

*Peter Frost leaning on a lamp post.*

On 1 November 1978 J Winter, director of Planning and Design, recommended to the City's Environmental Planning Committee that the rehabilitation and conversion of, say, ten of the remaining lamps was, "a small price to pay to secure the retention of features which add interest and beauty to the urban scene and which will be of increasing archaeological interest as time passes. The environment of a living city depends as much for its quality on a compendium of minor visual incidents, such as these sewer lamps, as upon major prestige buildings, and constant vigilance is necessary to ensure that this part of the City's heritage is not lost." In 1985, the Sheffield Council decided to refurbish and convert eighteen of these lamps to burn North Sea / natural gas for which they received a Civic Trust commendation.

These lamps remained lit 24 hours per day until in 1994, due to lack of resources, the Council terminated the gas supply contract and instructed the gas engineers to turn the lamps off at the lamp head. In 1997, the Nether Edge Neighbourhood Group, led by their chairman Peter Frost, with the help of Maurice Wilkinson and others, sought sponsorship to relight and maintain Nether Edge's two listed lamps. Following a generous donation from The Helen Roll Charity towards the £980 refurbishment costs, the lamps and a third lamp situated at the top of Stewart Rd., off Sharrowvale Rd. were relit. "It hasn't cost the council a penny", said Peter when interviewed leaning on a lamp by Martin Dawes for The Star, February 1998. He exploded the myth about the "sewer gas" lamps saying that they never ran off sewer gas and instead, "The lamps generated heat to produce convection currents which blew the gas away." Margaret Jakuboska, NENG's vice-chairman at the time added, "In the days when people shoved the stuff from earth closets into the sewers it meant the city could get pretty niffy. Long may these lamps continue shining on Nether Edge."

## Sources:

*The History of Webb Lamp Co.* www.xenophon.org.uk.
J. Winter's Report to Environmental Planning Committee 16th November 1978. Martin Dawes interview with Peter Frost, The Star newspaper, Monday, February 9, 1998.

# Part 7
# Entertainment

*Nether Edge Bowling Club*

# SNOOKER AT THE BOWLING CLUB

## Derek Agar

People come to live in Nether Edge for many reasons. Mine was snooker. My home town is Middlesbrough and I came to Sheffield University in the late 1960s. I chose Sheffield for three reasons: it had two first-division football teams (who were both relegated shortly after I arrived ...), the University was the only one at that time which did Anglo-Saxon translation in its English course and there was a picture of a nice swimming pool in the brochure. After I graduated I decided to apply for jobs in Middlesbrough and Sheffield and to take the first one I was offered, which happened to be the first I applied for, at King Ecgbert's School in Dore. I loved it there and stayed all my teaching life.

I had been playing league snooker for Meersbrook Bowling Club but, along with the talented Steve Clarke, was recruited by George Rudd in the late 1970s to come and play for Nether Edge Bowling Club. For me this was bliss, playing in a wonderful Victorian setting with 3 tables and the opportunity to play lots of frames in a room which Jimmy White's dad, Tommy, described as the best snooker room he had ever seen. When a breath of fresh air was needed we could stand on the balcony overlooking the green (allegedly the largest in Yorkshire) and appreciate what has been described as "Nether Edge's best-kept secret"

In the early 1980s Nether Edge BC had four snooker teams in the Sheffield Amateur Clubs League. The C and D teams were largely bowls players keeping together socially during the winter, the B team bounced between the A and B divisions, while gradually a very strong A team was being put together. Its most experienced members were Brian Agus (who took over

from George as captain) and Stewart Lale and they were joined by Tony Bristow, Brian Palmer, Brian Shanley, Steve Clarke, George Kita and me. A superb young

*Nether Edge BC A-team, winners of Cup and League Double 1984-5. Derek Agar on far left.*

player called Steve Darrington (brought up on Sandford Grove Road) joined us once he was old enough and later we were boosted by the hugely-talented Martin Lawrence, who knocked in regular centuries, including an unbeaten one in a cup final. When Brian retired as captain because of ill health he asked me to take over, and we stuck together for 20 years, winning 10 A-division titles and 11 Cups. Unfortunately this era of unprecedented success for the club and in the league's history ended when Stewart and George tragically died within 5 days of each other and in that same week I had a minor car crash which injured my neck and meant I had to give up league snooker.

The captain of the A team before me, Brian Agus, used to run the bar on the professional snooker circuit, including at the World Championships at Sheffield's Crucible, and as a result many of the players came to our club, the first being Jimmy White, who had mentioned to Brian that he couldn't find a suitable place to practice without being bothered and constantly asked for autographs. Brian sent him to us and he and his dad Tommy became great friends of the club. When the World Championships were on many of us were treated to playing practice frames with Jimmy, and we used to have fine sing-songs with Tommy, who often stayed in our club flat with Dave and Margaret Peate. Tommy was a dead ringer for Albert Steptoe and, like all Cockneys, he sang with his fingers after a preliminary build-up to a song.

Jimmy brought a variety of professionals with him to practice at our club, including Tony Drago and a very young Stephen Hendry. I was delighted

to score a practice session between Jimmy and Stephen (playing in a big baggy jumper), and after the 2-hour match the score was an amazing 7-7! Unfortunately that was the last we saw of Mr Hendry; there were rumours that his manager thought hanging around with Jimmy wasn't

*Steve Davis at Nether Edge Bowling Club 1981*

the best idea …

In the 1980s we also had a series of exhibition nights in the snooker room, again arranged by Brian Agus. Brian's family had a bookmaking business, and when it was taken over by Coral's, who sponsored the up-and-coming Steve Davis, part of the deal was that if and when he became world champion he would do 6 exhibition nights with the first one at Nether Edge BC. So our club was the first place Steve Davis played after becoming world champion! The two end tables were dismantled and scaffolded seating installed for the occasion. The seat numbers allocated for the occasion can still be seen on the permanent seating. Other professionals to do exhibition evenings in this era included Willie Thorne and Tony Jones. During this time Jimmy White was made an honorary member of the club, and he was very generous over the years with gifts of snooker equipment. Our steward Dave banned Jimmy's mate Ron Wood for inappropriate behaviour in the back bar. Dave didn't know who he was but a smile spread across his face when we pointed out that he had just thrown out a member of the Rolling Stones!

Our club celebrated its 150th anniversary in 2017, and I was honoured to be installed as President. The committee were magnificent in putting together a summer of celebrations which began in May with a Victorian-costume bowls match against Sheffield's other sesquicentennial club, Hallam Prop. There were garden parties, afternoon teas, croquet and scrabble events, a special quiz night, music nights from folk to skiffle, and finally a 150th celebration dinner at Baldwin's Omega. There are also now strong links with NENG and the Nether Edge Festival, with our own Richard Taylor at the forefront. Above the bar we now have a brilliant collective painting of the club and bowling green, done by our Art Group and complete with a 150th inscription.

Over many decades we have had lots of memorable characters, some of them sadly no longer with us, but remembered with great affection, not least for their eccentricities. There isn't time to mention them all here, but here are just a few glimpses from the snooker room.

George Rudd was the fearsome A-team captain two before me. He was actually a lovely man, but he ruled the snooker room with a rod of iron – he wore circular glasses with thin menacing frames, and one stare from George would turn a man into stone. If he suspected a member of having eaten crisps before coming up to the snooker room, that member was ordered to go and wash his hands before playing. Unfortunately, George's crowning moment came when he refereed the Steve Davis exhibition. Davis had potted a pink, George leaned over to re-spot it but it slipped out of his new silk gloves and bombarded the pack of reds, which flew everywhere. George then compounded his embarrassment by attempting to re-gather the reds. Apparently, the incident was mentioned in one of Davis's books, along the lines of "You'll never guess what happened in a northern club I went to" ...

Harry Bell was a legend in the snooker room. However, Harry's start at the club was a little unfortunate. When he first applied to join our club he asked if there was anything vital to remember for the protracted interview you had to have then. I advised him to make sure his shoes were clean, as they were the first part of you the rather Dickensian committee saw as you walked down the steps into the committee room. He dutifully cleaned his boots and passed his interrogation, then joined us in the snooker room to relax after his little ordeal. Halfway through the evening he set about following the second piece of advice, to take as many empty glasses as possible back down to the bar in order to set off well with Dave the steward. There were quite a few people in the room and therefore as Harry piled up the glasses he ended up with several stacks of them. As our hero attempted the turn on the stairs, his loss of control was confirmed by the loudest sound of shattering glass ever heard, together with the follow-up noises as the remaining intact glasses rolled agonisingly down the last few steps, only to shatter at the foot of the stairs. This was followed about 5 minutes afterwards by successive crashing noises as Harry swept the broken glass from each of the steps onto a scuttle.

At NEBC we had a lovely man called Mike Ruckledge, who was pure Oxbridge and refereed snooker in a sports jacket, cravat and silk gloves. After a player potted a red he would say in a rich baritone voice "Wan" rather than "One". When I joined Nether Edge BC from Meersbrook BC, encountering some of the old guard including Mike convinced me I had joined a club with more class, but it backfired on me the first time we played Meersbrook when one of my former team-mates enquired in a loud voice "Nah then Agar, who's t' p_____ in t' white gloves?"

The social aspects of the club have been boosted in recent years, not least by the infusion of new members, who are splendid people. We are very lucky to have such extensive and warm company. I hope and trust that the communal spirit not only in Nether Edge Bowling Club but in Nether Edge as a whole continues to flourish.

# BALDWINS OMEGA RESTAURANT

# Chris Venables

This chapter records the end of an era as Baldwins Omega has just closed and local residents are anxiously awaiting the site's fate. A planning application to demolish the restaurant and other buildings and erect 52 apartments in 6 blocks has been approved despite many objections concerning size and access.

In the 1700s the surrounding land was used for hunting by the grand houses of Hassop and Chatsworth and then, for several centuries, sandstone quarrying for building houses and making grinding stones and later for many of the gravestones in the Sheffield General Cemetery. Brincliffe Hall, an impressive building on the edge of the site was used by the Bluecoat School when they relocated from the city centre and built their own Bluecoats building on another part of the old quarry in 1911. During World War 1 there was a rifle range in the quarry and then it was used for landfill, the current car park being allegedly some 20 feet above the quarry floor.

By 1922 confectioner Mr John William Shaw, who lived in Arnold House at the top end of the site, had turned the old quarry into Brincliffe Tennis and Social Club described in a 1926 copy of "Lawn Tennis & Badminton" as "one of the best equipped clubs in the county - with nine excellent hard courts, with a spacious and well-equipped clubhouse. The latter has good dressing-rooms, luncheon and tea rooms, as well as a very fine ball-room...." The

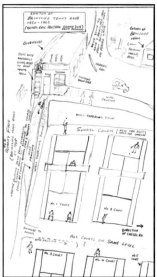

clubhouse (Brincliffe Hall) was hired out for social events until 1939 when the site was again requisitioned by the Army as a rifle range and the building became part of the drill hall for men stationed on Psalter Lane and close to an anti-aircraft battery due to its high elevation.

The success of public and private functions in the pavilion/Brincliffe Hall before and after WW2 led to the conversion of a former quarry building (to the left of the ramp out of the car-park) into a separate clubhouse, fitted out with changing rooms, kitchen and clubroom and external steps onto a flat roof as a viewing area over the tennis courts.

*Eric Renshaw's "Sketch of Brincliffe Tennis Club 1950-1962"*

Competition from other clubs and commercial considerations for the site led to the selling of Brincliffe Hall to Sheffield Refreshment Houses Ltd (who owned some of Sheffield's best hotels including Kenwood Hall, St Andrew's and Hunter House) and the closure of the tennis club. The new owners, wanting to build an ultra modern restaurant to rival London's finest, failed to get permission before demolishing Brincliffe Hall, a listed building, resulting in them being fined £800.

In September 1962, the new restaurant opened with a large dining room seating 140 and a sprung dance floor. It was called Omega, the last letter of the Greek alphabet, representing the ultimate or last word in fine  dining. The restaurant set out to provide atmosphere, service and food so its customers felt special right from the start with their welcome by the concierge and the parking of their Bentleys and Rolls-Royces by valets. The palatial surroundings included a hanging ceiling of laminated material, leather-backed seats and the use of silver cutlery manufactured in Sheffield. Customers were mainly from the business community, as, until the 1965 budget, business lunches were tax deductable and the "nouveau riche" were discovering the pleasures of fine food. After some success, trade declined so Sheffield Refreshment Houses closed the restaurant and sold the property to Stephen Hinchliffe in 1978.

In the mid '70s when working at Psalter Lane Art College (Sheffield Polytechnic and later, Sheffield Hallam University, Psalter Lane site), Ken Phillip remembers exploiting a direct line between Chelsea Road and the College. "This short journey (as well as dropping over a bank and wall into the College) took me through a delightful silver birch wood (on the edge of Omega's grounds) with a rusty rail track running through the trees to complete a circuit. The start and finish was by a large, solid, green painted hut which, it turned out, contained the paraphernalia to run the railway. Every so often a group of enthusiasts would descend on this wood, get up steam on the small scale locomotives and run them for the day giving rides to the small ones who, by some arcane method, had come to know 'steam up day'.

David Baldwin was brought up in Broomhall and attended Springfield School where domestic science was only for girls. After various short-lived jobs including working in the kitchens at the Nether Edge Hospital, he was employed as Omega's grill chef for about 18 months from 1963. He then ran several pubs including the Wheatsheaf at Parkhead, the Anglers Rest in Bamford and the Hillsborough Suite at Sheffield Wednesday's Football Ground, where he and his wife Pauline started developing their banqueting service, before buying and returning to the Omega (to be renamed Baldwins Omega) in 1981. To bolster the corporate business side, they started offering public events for sports and social clubs such as Salmon and Strawberry parties with covers for large numbers of people, then Caribbean evenings and charity themed events like Mardi Gras, disco nights and later Burns Night dinner dances. In the nineties, schools started using Baldwins Omega for their School Proms – a formal black tie occasion with Sixth Formers paying up to £26 to hire dinner jackets and trousers and £18 for a 3 -course meal of vegetable soup, chicken and profiteroles followed by a disco to celebrate finishing their schooldays. Visitors may remember Baldwins Omega winning Restaurant Loo of the Year 1999, after their son's firm installed space-age toilets with stainless steel "ice cream" cone urinals and moulded glass washbasins with push button taps, and even posher vanity units for the ladies.

In September 2016 and 2017, the Nether Edge Festival provided an opportunity for local residents to enjoy "an evening of fun and food" at Baldwins Omega with a welcoming drink and 3-course meal followed by musical entertainment, all for the special price of £20.

Following the retirement of David and Pauline Baldwin, Baldwins Omega closed on 21st July 2018 after nearly 40 years with them at its helm. Their head chef, operations manager and head waitress transferred to Abbeydale Sports Club to establish Omega at Abbeydale and continue the "Baldwins ethos of providing fresh food; presented to high standards and served with an attention to detail".

**Sources:**

*'Baldwins Omega The First 20 Years'*
www.sdlta.org.uk
https://omegaatabbeydale.co.uk/about

# TINTAGEL HOUSE & THE MERLIN THEATRE
## Kay Phillips

This account is based on notes from a conversation (in 1996) with Mary Boulton, a member of the Tintagel Trust, supplemented by additional research.

The large house adjacent to the Merlin Theatre has for many years been known as Tintagel House but in the early twentieth century it was named 'Meadow Bank'. It has had an interesting history and, for almost a century, its various owners have held a shared interest in the promotion of music and arts education.

*Tintagel House, formerly Meadow Bank.*

The first of these was Mr Wilfred Little Stephenson (1892-1975), a man whose life was a genuine 'rags to riches' story. Born in Staveley near Chesterfield into a working class family he went on to become a famous impresario, organising concerts across the country. Wilfred Stephenson's family was so poor that he had gone without shoes as a child and he left school at the age of twelve. He worked as a quarryman, miner and railway signalman before joining the Royal Engineers at the start of the First World War.

He began his career in entertainment by organising concerts for the church at Staveley –from which he pocketed the profits! Realising the potential of this activity, and the fact that it was preferable to manual work, he started to organise events more widely. Between 1921 and 1939 he organised 'celebrity subscription concerts' in 60 towns across Britain, especially in the Midlands. Many of the famous artists of that time were on his list. One example was Dame Clara Butt, who performed in Staveley and Chesterfield in 1921 before coming to Sheffield in 1922. Buses were often organised so that people could travel to see the performances. By the time War broke out in 1939 Wilfred was putting on 80 concerts a week.

It was said that he was not really interested in music, having no real knowledge of it, but was very astute in booking the best artists for his concerts. In just his third season of subscription concerts (1923) he was

**The People's Impresario**

the autobiography of
**Wilfred Stephenson**

edited and introduced by
**Celia de Piro**

*Cover of Wilfred Stephenson's Autobiography.*

offering a concert by the Royal Albert Hall Orchestra, conducted by Sir Edward Elgar. The following year Anna Pavlova performed with 60 ballet dancers and the London Symphony Orchestra conducted by Sir Thomas Beecham. He believed that music should be available to all, including the very young. School children could attend the performances for just a few pennies. He brought music of the highest quality to the masses and was dubbed 'The Woolworth of the Music World'. His autobiography appeared in a book titled 'The People's Impressario', edited and introduced by Celia de Piro.

Stephenson was a big, flamboyant man with a loud, 'fruity' voice according to local neighbours. He would entertain people at 'Meadow Bank' and was said to have taken advice from Sir Thomas Beecham to 'Surround yourself with beautiful things'. He changed the nature of the house, installing wood panelling and a new staircase. He also enlarged one room for music and created a library. He was reputed to have read only two books in his life but bought blocks of books to fill the shelves. The house also had extensive grounds which included a lake, on which there would be parties with lantern-lit boats. Some of the land was sold to the Kenwood Hotel in 1961. Stephenson played host to many famous musicians, partly because accommodating them was cheaper than paying for hotel rooms.

He later moved to number 4 Meadow Bank Road, building an extension to the house to accommodate his daughter. This coincided with the sale of the main house and the setting up of a new charity trust, Tintagel House Sheffield Ltd. There were some tensions between the Trust and Stephenson; he wasn't really in touch with their aims, although he continued to want to have a role in the running of it. Relations did improve in time. According to Mary Boulton, (one of the Trust members) he never really comprehended the charitable nature of its operations. The history of the Tintagel House Trust and its links to the earlier Sheffield Education Settlement warrants a little more explanation.

## Arnold Freeman and the Sheffield Education Settlement 1911- 1955

The Sheffield Education Settlement was begun by Arnold Freeman in 1911. He was a Fabian and an Oxford man; his network of friends and contacts included many of the intellectuals of that time, including George Bernard Shaw.

Freeman came to work at Shipton Street (near the old Sheffield Hospital) to educate the deprived. He gave lectures on art, classical history and other subjects. The premises were warm and he provided tea, so the lectures were always full of deprived people. From the start strong links were established with the new University of Sheffield and Freeman delivered lectures for the Workers Education Association (WEA) as part of his role.

In 1921 Arnold Freeman met Rudolph Steiner, the Austrian philosopher, social reformer and architect. From then on all of Freeman's lectures were influenced by Steiner's ideas. Art was seen as central to the educative process. A theatre was developed at Shipton Street so that plays could be staged and this was active until 1961. Freeman had retired in 1955 aged 69 and the Wardenship of the Education Settlement had been passed to Christopher Boulton, (Mary's husband) who renamed it 'The Steiner Foundation'.

## The Steiner Foundation and the Merlin Theatre 1955-1972

In the 1960s, under Christopher Boulton's leadership, the Steiner Foundation entered a new phase. A decision was taken to build a theatre in the grounds of the old house. The project was funded by a legacy of £100,000 from Christopher's aunt Julia. She had married an American millionaire and had been living in Paris before her death.

It would be an unusual design, based on Steiner's anthroposophical architectural principles. This influenced the interior layout, the angles of walls within the space and the shape and size of the windows. This was very much a hands-on project for Robert, Mary, her brother and sister-in-law, all of whom were involved in the Trust.

*The newly-completed Merlin Theatre in 1968*

Mary's brother took over the drawings and supervised the builder's workmen. They all helped to dig the foundations. The firm undertook to build the theatre without a quotation and were paid by results. The quality of the build was very good and the project was finished in 1968 at a cost of £80,000.

The first performance was Shakespeare's 'Henry V', on the 23rd April 1969. An advertisement placed in The Star invited actors, aged 16 or over, to audition. Approximately 70 people turned up but 30 women were quickly rejected as there were only three female parts. By contrast, all the male actors were successful because they could be given roles in the armies. Despite this early faux pas there followed many more Shakespeare plays, Greek theatre and other classics. The Merlin Theatre hosted eight opera groups in its early days; in time these amalgamated into South Yorkshire Opera. It was also a venue for local school concerts, poetry readings, music recitals, dance school concerts and lectures. Mary recalled that, 'There was a wonderful atmosphere at that time, there were so many people using the building.'

Christopher Boulton had seen the completion of the building but sadly he died in 1972. Robert Chamberlain then took on the management of the Tintagel facilities. In 1984 a small pre-school nursery was opened in the theatre building and many local children attended, taking advantage of the lovely grounds as well as the indoor space. A few years later the nursery closed and a Steiner School was established. Although this was initially quite successful it was short-lived. According to Mary Boulton, 'it failed because it was too costly to run and needed to be bigger in order to balance the books, but the building was too small for it to be viable'.

The refurbished Merlin Theatre today

By the early 21st Century the fabric of the Theatre had deteriorated and it eventually had to be closed for five years because of flood damage. Fortunately, after a successful fundraising campaign, it was completely refurbished and reopened in 2015 as a bright, modern facility. It is once again in regular use by schools, choirs and other community groups.

Tintagel House and the Merlin Theatre are now part of the Ruskin Mill Trust's facilities. The buildings are managed and run by Freeman College and Brantwood Specialist School, providing education and residential care for young people with a range of special needs.

---

# ABBEYDALE PICTURE HOUSE

## Mike Higginbottom

The Abbeydale Picture House was and still is Sheffield's most splendid suburban cinema. Two of the original directors purchased the empty site on Abbeydale Road from Sheffield Corporation for £1,700 towards the end of the First World War, and the Abbeydale Picture House Co. Ltd was registered on June 21st 1919. The Board consisted of a cinematograph exhibitor,

*The Abbeydale Picture House. Photo; Granola*

Matthew Fordyce Smart, and a grocer, an engineer, a stockbroker, a draughtsman, an insurance manager and a builder and contractor. This was a common pattern – local men with money to spare enlisting a cinema-industry professional to capitalise on the demand for movie entertainment as peace returned.

The directors commissioned a Newcastle architect, Pascal J Steinlet, to design a landmark building, clearly visible from a distance, clad in white faience with a prominent dome. Pascal Steinlet had built cinemas in the north-east before the War, and was resuming his practice after his return from war service. At the time he designed the Abbeydale, his practice was a partnership with Henry Selwyn Dixon, and they delegated the local supervision of the building to a Sheffield architect, Arthur Whitaker. Pascal Stienlet went on to design the splendid Majestic Cinema in Leeds City Square in 1922, and returned to Sheffield in 1927 when he was responsible for the

Manor Picture House at the top of Prince of Wales Road.

The Abbeydale is unusual among Sheffield's suburban cinemas for its generous stage-provision, complete with a fly-tower and three storeys of dressing-rooms. The front-of-house area included café facilities and the graded site allowed for a ballroom beneath the auditorium rake and a snooker hall beneath the stage. Dixon & Steinlet's original plans intended 1,200 seats in the pit and a further 600 in the circle, but the cinema opened with an advertised capacity of 1,350.

It became clear that, in the face of post-war inflation, the original working capital of £50,000 would be insufficient. The directors issued a second prospectus in September 1920, increasing the nominal capital to £75,000, though it seems that the subscribed shares never exceeded £62,000. This further prospectus mentions "a splendid organ" – a curious change of plan. Pascal Steinlet's design made no provision for an organ chamber anywhere around the proscenium, and an unsigned plan stamped October 22nd 1920 shows an organ positioned downstage centre immediately behind the screen, rendering the stage tower unusable for live performances.

In a rush to generate revenue, the directors invited the Lord Mayor, Alderman W F Wardley, to open the picture house at a charity matinée on the afternoon of December 20th 1920. The Lord Mayor, "*hoped that a high standard of film would always form the feature of the programme*", remarking that "*in some of the lower-class houses in the city films were shown which he did not think had been seen by the Censor.*" The main feature was a costume romance, 'The Call of the Road', starring the British actor Victor McLaglen. The manager was Mr S Taylor Farrell, and the ten-piece orchestra was directed by Meersbrook-born Arnold Bagshaw. There was, as yet, no organ: indeed, the café, ballroom and snooker hall were all incomplete.

The following day's Sheffield Independent gave a perfunctory description of the auditorium: the décor was pale and deep cream with gold and the mahogany seats were upholstered in green velvet. "*At the side of the screen [were] two Doric pillars [actually Ionic] and at the top a chaste panel of Grecian figures on a background of pale blue*".

Opening the building simply as a picture hall proved insufficient to keep the company afloat. By June 1921 the original directors had resigned, and were replaced by a more experienced board which already operated the Star Cinema on Ecclesall Road and later opened the Central Cinema on The Moor in 1922. The new company secretary was Edwin Ransom Harrison, an accountant who went on to become chairman of the Rover Motor Company. The cinema expertise was provided by Isaac Graham, who gave his address as the Grand Hotel, Sheffield. The rest of the board consisted of a stockbroker and two fruit merchants. The new board quickly arranged debentures amounting to at least £25,000 in order to open the café on September 5th 1921, the ballroom on September 30th and the twelve-table billiard hall on October 17th.

They ordered from the Sheffield organ-builder Brindley & Co of Suffolk Road, a two-manual "Clavorchester" pipe-organ, specifically designed to accompany silent films with a range of atmospheric stops imitating orchestral instruments. This "Great Organ" was inaugurated on three days beginning October 31st 1921 by the organist of the Central Hall, Westminster, Arthur Meale FRCO, whose celebrated tone-poem, 'The Storm' was, according to the Sheffield Telegraph, *"played with realistic effect, [and] received with very hearty appreciation".* Arnold Bagshaw, as musical director, acted as organist until he transferred to the Central Picture House when it opened in 1922. He was succeeded by the eighteen-year-old Harold Coombes, celebrated for the red spats he wore to make his footwork visible to the audience. Harold Coombes had begun his professional career at the age of eleven as assistant organist at St Oswald's Church, Millhouses, and in 1919 became organist at St Paul's Church, Norton Lees. He began broadcasting on the Sheffield-based 6FL BBC station which opened in 1923. He left Sheffield in 1933 to work in Aberdeen and then Bournemouth, where his lively performances earned him the nickname *"Bouncing Harold".*

In 1928 the Abbeydale directors, anticipating increased competition with the approach of talking pictures, asked Arthur Whitaker to rearrange the stage to allow cine-variety performances. The organ was moved upstage where it was barely audible. Harold Coombes' successor, Douglas Scott, complained, *"the volume was poor, due to the fact that the organ chambers were placed as far back as possible on the stage and…at least 20% of the sound went through the stage roof. The screen and tabs absorbed much of the remaining volume and when the safety curtain was lowered nothing could be heard in the theatre."*

On the last day of 1928 the new combined programme of films and live variety acts was launched: "OPENING OF NEW STAGE!! ENORMOUS ATTRACTION!!!" The feature film, 'A Woman on Trial' starring Pola Negri, was supported by the Q's, "a new-style Episode Show" from the London

Coliseum, with "a cast of 10 Brilliant Burlesquers, headed by Mabel Sylvester and Charles Hutchins". This pattern continued, billed as 'Abbeydale Cine-Variety', for the next couple of years. In January 1930, by which time many Sheffield cinemas were showing talking pictures, the Abbeydale booked film star Gibb McLaughlin for a week of personal appearances, accompanied for the first three days by his film 'The Silent House', in which he starred as Dr Chan Fu the sinister Chinese Mandarin.

The transition to sound films was accomplished over a weekend, March 8th-9th 1930, and the first programme – 'all-talking and singing with colour sequences' – featured Janet Gaynor in 'Sunny Side Up'. Variety turns abruptly ceased, though Douglas Scott continued trying to make himself heard as organist until 1940.

The Abbeydale Picture House Co Ltd eventually paid its first dividend, 2½%, in 1931, and through the 1930s and the Second World War the building at last fulfilled its potential, offering films, dancing and snooker to an appreciative clientele drawn from Nether Edge and the length of the Millhouses tram-route. Abbeydale Road was badly hit on the night of the Thursday Blitz, December 12th 1940. The film, 'Young Tom Edison' with Mickey Rooney, was stopped soon after 6pm and the audience sheltered in the ballroom, with others who found their way through the streets, until 4am. Shirley Rae (née White) recalled that the ballroom floor was packed 'like sardines' and the only available drinking water dripped from a single tap where people queued to wet their lips from the same cup. Phil Lovell remembers that his dad was inside. He had to fight his way out to be with his family who lived at the top of Broadfield Rd. The building sustained minor damage, and reopened on Boxing Day 1940, showing films only in the afternoon because of the blackout and the shortage of public transport. Oral reminiscences of the period immediately before and during the Second World War tell that the Abbeydale had a happy atmosphere for patrons and staff.

Television reached South Yorkshire in October 1951, and many households bought sets to watch the Coronation on June 2nd 1953. The film industry responded by providing visual experiences unavailable at home – particularly colour and wide-screen formats. The original proscenium, too narrow for Cinemascope, was hidden behind a bigger, plain proscenium and the panoramic screen was installed over a single weekend by the chief operator, Harry Holmes. The relief of Grecian figures has remained out of sight ever since.

In April 1955 the Leeds-based Star Cinemas (London) Ltd took over the licences of the Abbeydale, Star and Wicker cinemas. At the Abbeydale this new ownership brought radical change within a matter of days. The Abbeydale opened for its first ever Sunday performance, 'Theirs is the Glory' on April 24th and the day after presented the first CinemaScope film, 'Seven Brides for Seven Brothers'. Soon afterwards, according to his son, the chief operator, Harry Holmes, told the new management, "Do you know what you can do? You can take my notice."

Later that year the billiard hall was converted into a club and restaurant and leased to the Abbeydale Propriety Club. Star Cinemas worked hard to maintain cinema audiences with a range of publicity stunts. Fess Parker, the Hollywood star of Davy Crockett, King of the Wild Frontier, made a personal appearance on April 13th 1956. The Johnny Dankworth Orchestra appeared at the Abbeydale in May 1957; there was wrestling in October 1959 and two performances of the ballet Coppelia in December 1959. The management apparently cut corners where they thought they could: the manager was prosecuted and fined in 1958 for having only three attendants to supervise a Sunday audience of over a thousand. The customary practice had been to close either the stalls or the circle if there was insufficient front-of-house staff to cover both areas.

Until the end of the 1950s the queues under the glazed marquee stretched past Mr Poppleton's sweet shop, "Pop's", on the corner into Bedale Road. By the early 1960s it was usually possible to walk straight in and buy a ticket. The other street attractions for nights at the pictures were the chip shop and Mr Phillipson's Temperance Bar at 377 Abbeydale Road, a favourite of lads big enough to buy a 6d pint of sarsaparilla but not old enough to take a chance in a pub. The other local cinemas shut one after another and when the Heeley Palace closed down in 1965, only the Abbeydale was left showing films. The only time that bingo came to the Abbeydale was a five-week period of Sunday-afternoon sessions from Christmas 1961 while the Star was being converted to bingo; the ballroom was used for bingo for a period in 1964.

The place was beginning to show its age: Bill Allerton, who knew it from the late 1950s, describes its atmosphere as *"muted grandeur."* Helen Burgess remembers it in the early 1970s and recognised that *"it must have been a very plush cinema [that] attracted audiences from Nether Edge and Millhouses" but was "past its best…almost as if it had given up on itself".*

Programmes targeted minority audiences, and there was a walkout when the feature was Ken Russell's violent and sexually explicit film, 'The Devils'. In the miserable winter of the three-day week during the 1974 Miners' Strike the cinema opened intermittently and there was no heating. Groups of students used to meet at the Broadfield Tavern, buy bottles of wine and take fur coats and blankets into the freezing balcony of the Abbeydale. From October 1974 the stalls was closed to the public, and the last film – Charles Bronson in Breakout, with Lords of Flatbush – was shown on Saturday July 5th 1975. By then only two other suburban cinemas were operating in Sheffield – the Rex at Intake and the Vogue (previously the Essoldo and originally the Capitol) at Sheffield Lane Top.

Abbeydale Picture House used as an office equipment showroom for A. & F. Drake Ltd., 1988.

*Inside A & F Drake Ltd + safety curtain (photo: Harry Rigby 2004)*

Since it went dark the Abbeydale has been singularly fortunate in its owners. The office-equipment dealers, A & F Drake Ltd, previously of Cambridge Street in the city-centre, bought it for showroom and warehouse space, declaring that its landmark status served as an advertisement for the business. Once the seating, projectors and screen were removed, the physical adaptations were minimal: the balcony was enclosed by a drop wall and suspended ceiling; partitions divided the rear stalls and the stage was jacked up to double the available floor space within the fly tower. This meant that only the bottom half of the safety curtain was visible from the auditorium.

The ballroom continued to operate as the Kay Gee Bee night club, and subsequently promoted Northern Soul disco until 1983 when the sprung dance floor was replaced by concrete to support snooker tables. The Abbeydale was one of only two Sheffield cinemas to be listed Grade II in

August 1989. (The other is the Adelphi, Attercliffe.) When A & F Drake Ltd ceased trading late in 1991, the snooker club continued in the basement. Proposals for the former cinema included conversion to a mosque (see Mohammed Nazir's memories) or a church but the building remained empty for over a

*In need of restoration*

decade until the Friends of the Abbeydale Picture House took it over to run drama schools and performances for young people in 2005.

The Friends' project came to an end and the building was sold in 2012 to Phil Robins, the owner of The Edge climbing centre on Bramall Lane. He intended to convert it to a climbing centre, and removed the partitions, drop wall and suspended ceiling that Drakes had installed, revealing the entire space of the auditorium for the first time since 1976. Due to the opening of various other climbing walls in the area, Phil decided instead to use the Abbeydale as a multipurpose community venue in conjunction with local events such as the Antiques Quarter Vintage Markets.

*Hand Of,* an arts platform led by Rob Hughes and Louise Snape, conceived the idea of a Picture House Revival weekend in July 2015 to commemorate the fortieth anniversary of the last film-show. They installed stalls seating and a screen, borrowed projectors from the Projected Picture Trust, arranged bars, food-stalls, popcorn and sarsaparilla and presented, among other films, a 35mm print of 'The Call of the Road', the first movie ever shown in the building in December 1920, with a live piano accompaniment.

They followed this success with a year of film and other arts events and proved the building's potential as a modern entertainment space. The rear stalls area was converted into a café-bar and kitchen space, and the operating box was rewired for the Projected Picture Trust to install 35mm projectors on long-term loan.

*Flea market stalls inside Abbeydale Picture House*

*Showing of "The Call of the Road" by Hand Of 18-19 July 2015. Abbeydale Picture House*

The charity CADS (Creative Arts Development Space) took a 25-year lease of the Abbeydale Picture House in January 2017 in order to develop and restore the building and secure its future. As it approaches its centenary, the Abbeydale Picture House is blessed by the vision and imagination of enthusiastic supporters and the backing of the local community, so that once again the building does what it was designed to do – make people happy.

Thanks to Sam Manning and Richard Miles for assistance with this article, which is based on original research by Dr Clifford H Shaw, with material from oral history interviews by Holly Dann.

---

# BOOTH UNWIN, SINGER

## Peter Machan

I wonder if anyone remembers Booth Unwin, the renowned bass singer who was a stalwart of the choir at St Peter's, Abbeydale throughout the 50s and 60s? During the early years of the 1960s I was head chorister at St Peter's and the choir, led by the organist Cyril Fawcett, who ran a builder's merchants on nearby Hale Street, was well regarded. When my voice broke it was Booth Unwin who taught me to sing from the bass clef, which I still do today as a member of Escafeld Choral Society.

St Peter's choristers, 1948

I fondly remember Booth Unwin, who was a bank manager, and looked in later life something like Captain Mainwaring in Dad's Army. He lived on Machon Bank, below Nether Edge. I was reminded of him recently on discovering the photograph of him below in the programme of concerts of the Sheffield Choral Union of 1927, in which he was one of the soloists in Elgar's 'The Apostles' performed at the Victoria Hall, and conducted by the great Sheffield chorus master, Sir Henry Coward, whose house on Kenwood Bank is marked by a blue plaque.

The reviews accompanying the photograph are as follows;-

*"The voice of Mr Unwin, the bass-baritone, is one which is very singular in strength, full and steady. He claimed the unhesitating approval of the audience"*        Bristol Times and Mirror.

*"To the bass, Mr Booth Unwin, perhaps fell the most praise. A young singer with a wide experience, his performance was as near perfection as possible"* Barnoldswick and Earby Times.

*"The outstanding performance of the evening was the impersonation of Elijah by Mr Booth Unwin. It was a magnificent vocal and interpretive effort"* –Sheffield Telegraph.

Clearly he went on to extend his repertoire for I have found that he sang

Mr. BOOTH UNWIN.

in various music programmes on the BBC during the 1950s and appeared in seaside summer shows. It is recorded that he was well known for his rendition of Mussorgsky's 'The Song of the Flea'! The respect in which he was held by the musical fraternity is shown by his serving as Secretary to the Northern Branch of the Incorporated Society of Musicians. The love of music clearly ran in the family as his sister Bessie was a soprano soloist and musical director. Booth Unwin died in May 1966 and I sang at his funeral at St Peter's.

# Part 8

## SCANDAL & SENSATION IN

## VICTORIAN NETHER EDGE

# A Scandalous Divorce

On census night 1871, there lived at 12 Kenwood Road one Thomas Newton, aged 46, partner in Francis Newton and Sons of Portobello Works (cutlery manufacturers and employers of 45 men), with his wife and their nine year old son, also named Thomas, and one female servant. A normal enough middle class family of the time, you may think, if perhaps a bit smaller than usual. But behind that respectable Kenwood Park façade lay an altogether different story which was far from respectable.

Thomas came from a well-established Sheffield business family. If the name Francis Newton sounds familiar it might be because there is a Wetherspoons pub of that name at the top of Clarkehouse Road in Broomhall. In an attempt at heritage marketing the company named it after Thomas's father, whose house it originally was, and here Thomas was born in 1825. He married, and moved out to a house on Western Bank, where unfortunately his wife died aged only 22. But Newton & Sons thrived, and in due course, after serving as Master Cutler and receiving the plaudits of his peers Francis retired in 1854, leaving the business to his three sons.

Then, on a business trip to Birmingham in about 1857, Thomas became acquainted with 19 year old Rhoda Baylis Hall, who came from Bilston. He was not the first businessman travelling away from home to pass his time with a young lady of easy virtue, and he was, after all, single. But this was different. He brought Rhoda back to Sheffield, and on 14 November 1857 at St Philips Church he married her, and brought her to live in Nether Edge (or rather, Sharrow as it was then known), first at Kenwood Road, and later at Clintock Place, Wostenholm Road, next door to the doctor's house, Rock House.

Fairytale prince and pauper romance, or life-changing blunder? Thomas's lawyer Dr Deane laid the matter before the jury with blunt eloquence. 'It was no good mincing the words: she was upon the town, and off the town he took her, and raised her to the position of his wife...and, he must tell the Jury, lived with her before the marriage'.

So in June 1861 the romance ended up in the Divorce Court in London. Only in 1858 had civil divorce become possible, with adultery as the sole ground on which men could divorce their wives, while wives had to prove adultery with additional aggravations such as cruelty or desertion. Thomas's lawyers therefore devoted their efforts to building up a squalid picture of Rhoda's life in Sheffield, especially during Thomas's many absences on business, when, they argued, she had slipped back into her old ways. Attention focused on her relationship with three men: Henry Whitfield - according to Dr Deane 'a low professional singer, a person who went about and sang at casinos and public houses and places of that sort' – Walter Frith, aged 24, who lived at Broomgrove and was a partner in his father's optician's business; and 27 year old Peter Ibbotson, who worked in his father Thomas's cutlery business and also lived in Broomhall. Adultery was alleged with Whitfield and Frith, both in the matrimonial home and at Whitfield's lodgings; they were cited as co-respondents. Evidence was produced of Rhoda's visits to a 'gay house' – a brothel – in Eyre Lane, and to the Reuben's Head pub on Burgess Street, frequented, so said the cabman who drove her there with Frith, by 'ladies and gentlemen...I have seen ladies and gentlemen going up and coming down stairs'.

On getting wind of all this Thomas had sent Rhoda back to her family in Bilston, but she returned, climbing in through the bedroom window on a ladder. Then he brought in trusted servants to take charge of the household, and Rhoda, during his absences, but to little effect. One of them, Sarah Anne Elliott, a farmer's daughter from Penistone, testified to Rhoda's state of undress with Whitfield in her bedroom – and, indeed, in her bed – to her going upstairs with Frith, and to her late-night absences in his company. Damningly, letters were produced from Rhoda to Thomas begging him to forgive her and not to divorce her; as adultery was the only grounds for divorce, that might, as the judge pointed out, be construed as an admission of guilt.

Against this barrage Rhoda's and the co-respondents' lawyers could produce little ammunition. Rhoda accused Thomas of adultery with Mrs Frances Hague, the wife of a business associate, but no evidence was produced. They attempted to discredit the witness Elliott with an alleged relationship with Ibbotson, and pointed out that much of the evidence was circumstantial and depended on assumptions

*12 Kenwood Road*

that could not be proved. Of the co-respondents, Frith did not help his own case by trying to excuse himself on the grounds that Rhoda was the kind of person 'with whom any man so disposed might form this kind of connection', and that he shouldn't have to pay costs because of her previous lifestyle. Whitfield was nowhere to be seen. The judge's summing up was heavily weighted against Rhoda, and the jury had only to 'put their heads together for a moment' to bring in a verdict of guilty of adultery against her. As the Judge said, awarding a decree nisi, she had 'thrown away the chance afforded her of becoming a respectable woman'. The chances of such a woman winning a case such as this were surely negligible.

Thomas, wisely perhaps, left the neighbourhood and went to live in Handsworth. But the story has a final twist. On 6 February 1865, at Oxford Place Methodist Chapel in Leeds, Thomas was married for the third time – to none other than Sarah Anne Elliott, his former servant, who had given evidence on his behalf in the divorce trial. And when he brought her back to Sheffield to live on Kenwood Road they were accompanied by their son, Thomas Elliott Newton, born in Derby in 1862, barely a year after the divorce case, and three years before his parents married. Sadly, Sarah Anne died in 1878: whatever else you may say about him, Thomas was not lucky in love. He moved to Broomgrove Road with his son and daughter in law, and died in 1892. And what of the unfortunate Rhoda? A Rhoda Newton, aged 43 died in Birmingham in 1880. Other than that, no further trace can be found.

# The Workhouse Master and the Landlord's Daughter

The Union Inn, built in the early 1840s by the Boot family of builders and quarry owners stood as it still stands on Cherrytree Hill, only a short stroll from the newly-built Ecclesall Workhouse. In 1867 at Leeds Assizes Joseph Boot, landlord of the Union since 1842, sued Charles Shentall, the 28 year old Master of the Workhouse, for seducing his daughter, Emma Ann, also 28.

Charles was a frequent visitor to the pub – the Workhouse was hardly a fun place to spend the evening. He played whist with Joseph, no doubt taking a drink or two, and frequently stayed late. He became close to Emma, who also visited him at the Workhouse (only twice, she said), and after a year or so the Boots came to regard Charles as Emma's fiancé – almost one of the family. But then, in Emma's delicately-chosen words, 'I was thrown a good deal into his company, and at last I had a child by him'.

Discovering his daughter's condition Joseph stormed down to the Workhouse accompanied by Emma and one of her brothers and demanded that Charles marry her. I can't, protested Charles, my employers – the Poor Law Guardians – won't let me marry. Joseph did not believe him, and left Emma to plead her case, but to no avail. The child, named Lydia, was born at the Union in August 1866 and was sent to a wet-nurse at Loxley, but sadly only lived a few weeks.

You could sue people in those days for seducing your grown-up daughter. It was assumed she had household duties – Emma served behind the bar – so her father was entitled to compensation if deprived of her services. If you think this meant she was regarded as virtually the property of her father (until she became the property of a husband), you would be right.

In court, Charles insisted there had been no talk of marriage. He and Emma had openly canoodled in the presence of her parents (she sat on his knee!), who often went to bed leaving the couple alone together downstairs in the pub, and they knew all about her late-night visits to the Workhouse. Would a respectable father allow such intimacy? Moreover, it emerged, Emma had a past: she had been pregnant before, in 1862, by one John Kirby, of Sheaf Island Brewery, a man in his sixties who lived in a big house nearby. Money had been demanded of him and after pleading poverty he duly paid up. The child was still-born. It was alleged that she had been pregnant by Kirby previously, in 1860, when money had also been paid. There was talk of others. So was Charles really a wicked seducer, or was he, in his lawyer's words, 'an unfortunate man [who] had formed a connection with a girl of loose habits'? And shouldn't Emma's father, failing to control his daughter's behaviour, have 'endeavoured to hide her disgrace from the world' instead of 'parading her infamy in order to make money by it'?

The jury took only fifteen minutes to award Joseph £40 – well below the £100 he demanded, but with costs of over £200 still too much for Charles, who lost his job at the Workhouse and immediately declared himself bankrupt. Joseph never got his £40. By the end of the year he had left the pub he ran for 25 years, and after his death in 1880 the Boots sold it to Tennants Brewery. Charles moved to Brincliffe Edge Road, became a valuer and estate agent, and eventually a brewery manager and a stalwart of the Conservative Party. He died in 1886 aged only 46, having, it seems, never married. In 1872 Emma married a man from Nottingham and, we hope, lived happily ever after. And as for poor little Lydia, next time you raise a glass of Gareth and Sarah's finest, think of her. She may have begun her short life near where you are sitting.

# 'Quackery On Stilts' at the Union Hotel

Madame Enault, curer of incurable diseases, purveyor of miracle medicines, and expert extractor of teeth, arrived on Cherrytree Hill in July 1880, resplendent in scarlet, velvet and gold, her gilt caravan drawn by three magnificent horses with nodding plumes, and accompanied by an execrably tuneless brass band. She took up residence at the Union Hotel, where she held court every morning to a huge crowd of the afflicted – or rather, to those of the afflicted who had managed to get hold of one of the tickets which she threw among them as they surged around the pub and its environs. 'Women screamed,' reported the Sheffield Independent. 'cripples besought strong ruffians for mercy, or at least fair play, and in a few moments the fifteen tickets were in the possession of the hale and hearty, who trafficked with them amongst the lame and decrepit' for as much as 2s 6d each.

*The Union Hotel, 1890s.*

In the afternoons, Madame proceeded in her caravan, past cheering crowds along Cemetery Road and the Moor, to the parade ground on Matilda Street, where before a crowd of ten to fifteen thousand people (and accompanied by her band) she pulled teeth, sold her patent medicines, railed against her critics in the local press and, supposedly, cured the incurable.  Teeth-pulling, as the Independent observed, is no great accomplishment to those possessed of a strong wrist; her 'China Caustic' and 'Indian Balm', which she said derived extraordinary curative powers from over 200 exotic herbs, were found by a local analytical chemist to contain no significant active ingredients; and as for miracle cures, the truly afflicted seemed to get overlooked when she left the parade ground and drove off back to the Union.  Despite hints that she would stay longer, lease a house in Kenwood Park perhaps, no convincing miracles had been reported before she abruptly left Sheffield at the crack of dawn in the direction of Huddersfield – or perhaps Halifax - after a stay of only a week.

Enault was Italian – or was she French, or Belgian?  She had medical degrees from several great European universities - or, more likely, none. She had travelled in America, where she was (or was not) hailed as a miracle worker, and arrived in Sheffield via Liverpool, Warrington, St Helens and Birmingham, leaving disappointed clients in those places who had paid for, but not received, their miracle cures.  The press estimated that she must have raked in fifty to a hundred pounds a day on the parade ground.  This 'quackery on stilts' as the Independent put it, had revealed that 'many of the Sheffield people are less sharp than they should be' and made her several hundred pounds richer for the discovery.  She offered cruelly false hope to the afflicted, in an age when medical cures were less dependable than they are today.  But to the rest of Sheffield she offered  something to gawk at and cheer, quackery or no quackery.  She was a spectacle, albeit a transient one, and for a short week she made Cherrytree Hill and the Union the centre of Sheffield's attention.

John Baxendale

Montgomery Road, Sheffield

...wood Lodge, Sharrow

G.B.& Sons Ltd

Moncrieffe Road Netheredge.